Triumph
TR6 (1968-76)

Your Expert Guide
To common problems & how to fix them

Triumph TR6, all models
(1968-76)

Your marque expert
Paul Hogan

Other great books from Veloce –

Handbooks

Caring for your car – How to maintain & service your car (Fry)
Caring for your car's bodywork and interior (Nixon)
Caring for your bicycle – How to maintain & repair your bicycle (Henshaw)
Caring for your scooter – How to maintain & service your 49cc to 125cc twist & go scooter (Fry)
Efficient Driver's Handbook, The (Moss)
Electric Cars – The Future is Now! (Linde)
First aid for your car – Your expert guide to common problems & how to fix them (Collins)
How your car works (Linde)
How your motorcycle works – Your guide to the components & systems of modern motorcycles (Henshaw)
Motorcycles – A first-time-buyer's guide (Henshaw)
Motorhomes – A first-time-buyer's guide (Fry)
Pass the MoT test! – How to check & prepare your car for the annual MoT test (Paxton)
Selling your car – How to make your car look great and how to sell it fast (Knight)
Simple fixes for your car – How to do small jobs for yourself and save money (Collins)

Expert Guides

Land Rover Series I-III – Your expert guide to common problems & how to fix them (Thurman)
MG Midget & A-H Sprite – Your expert guide to common problems & how to fix them (Horler)

SpeedPro Series

4-Cylinder Engine Short Block High-Performance Manual – New Updated & Revised Edition (Hammill)
Aerodynamics of Your Road Car, Modifying the (Edgar and Barnard)
Alfa Romeo DOHC High-performance Manual (Kartalamakis)
Alfa Romeo V6 Engine High-performance Manual
(Kartalamakis)
BMC 998cc A-series Engine, How to Power Tune (Hammill)
1275cc A-series High-performance Manual (Hammill)
Camshafts – How to Choose & Time Them For Maximum Power (Hammill)
Competition Car Datalogging Manual, The (Templeman)
Custom Air Suspension – How to install air suspension in your road car – on a budget! (Edgar)
Cylinder Heads, How to Build, Modify & Power Tune – Updated & Revised Edition (Burgess & Gollan)
Distributor-type Ignition Systems, How to Build & Power Tune – New 3rd Edition (Hammill)
Fast Road Car, How to Plan and Build – Revised & Updated Colour New Edition (Stapleton)
Ford SOHC 'Pinto' & Sierra Cosworth DOHC Engines, How to Power Tune – Updated & Enlarged Edition (Hammill)
Ford V8, How to Power Tune Small Block Engines (Hammill)
Harley-Davidson Evolution Engines, How to Build & Power Tune (Hammill)
Holley Carburetors, How to Build & Power Tune – Revised & Updated Edition (Hammill)
Honda Civic Type R High-Performance Manual, The (Cowland & Clifford)
Jaguar XK Engines, How to Power Tune – Revised & Updated Colour Edition (Hammill)
Land Rover Discovery, Defender & Range Rover – How to Modify Coil Sprung Models for High Performance & Off-Road Action (Hosier)
MG Midget & Austin-Healey Sprite, How to Power Tune – Enlarged & updated 4th Edition (Stapleton)
MGB 4-Cylinder Engine, How to Power Tune (Burgess)
MGB V8 Power, How to Give Your – Third Colour Edition (Williams)
MGB, MGC & MGB V8, How to Improve – New 2nd Edition (Williams)

Mini Engines, How to Power Tune On a Small Budget – Colour Edition (Hammill)
Motorcycle-engined Racing Cars, How to Build (Pashley)
Motorsport, Getting Started in (Collins)
Nissan GT-R High-performance Manual, The (Gorodji)
Nitrous Oxide High-performance Manual, The (Langfield)
Optimising Car Performance Modifications (Edgar)
Race & Trackday Driving Techniques (Hornsey)
Retro or classic car for high performance, How to modify your (Stapleton)
Rover V8 Engines, How to Power Tune (Hammill)
Secrets of Speed – Today's techniques for 4-stroke engine blueprinting & tuning (Swager)
Sportscar & Kitcar Suspension & Brakes, How to Build & Modify – Revised 3rd Edition (Hammill)
SU Carburettor High-performance Manual (Hammill)
Successful Low-Cost Rally Car, How to Build a (Young)
Suzuki 4x4, How to Modify For Serious Off-road Action (Richardson)
Tiger Avon Sportscar, How to Build Your Own – Updated & Revised 2nd Edition (Dudley)
Triumph TR2, 3 & TR4, How to Improve (Williams)
Triumph TR5, 250 & TR6, How to Improve (Williams)
Triumph TR7 & TR8, How to Improve (Williams)
Triumph V8 Engine, How to Build a Short Block For High Performance (Hammill)
Volkswagen Beetle Suspension, Brakes & Chassis, How to Modify For High Performance (Hale)
Volkswagen Bus Suspension, Brakes & Chassis for High Performance, How to Modify – Updated & Enlarged New Edition (Hale)
Weber DCOE, & Dellorto DHLA Carburetors, How to Build & Power Tune – 3rd Edition (Hammill)

Workshop Pro Series

Car Electrical and Electronic Systems (Edgar)
Modifying the Electronics of Modern Classic Cars (Edgar)

Setting up a Home Car Workshop (Edgar)

Enthusiast's Restoration Manual Series

Beginner's Guide to Classic Motorcycle Restoration, The (Burns)
Citroën 2CV Restore (Porter)
Classic Car Electrical Systems (Astley)
Classic Car Bodywork, How to Restore (Thaddeus)
Classic Car Electrics (Thaddeus)
Classic Car Suspension, Steering & Wheels, How to Restore & Improve (Parish – translator)
Classic Cars, How to Paint (Thaddeus)
Classic Large Frame Vespa Scooters, How to Restore
Classic Small Frame Vespa Scooters, How to Restore (Paxton)
Ducati Bevel Twins 1971 to 1986 (Falloon)
Classic Off-road Motorcycles, How to Restore (Burns)
Honda CX500 & CX650, How to restore – YOUR step-by-step colour illustrated guide to complete restoration (Burns)
Honda Fours, How to restore – YOUR step-by-step colour illustrated guide to complete restoration (Burns)
Jaguar E-type (Crespin)
Kawasaki Z1, Z/KZ900 & Z/KZ1000, How to restore (Rooke)
Reliant Regal, How to Restore (Payne)
Triumph TR2, 3, 3A, 4 & 4A, How to Restore (Williams)
Triumph TR5/250 & 6, How to Restore (Williams)
Triumph TR7/8, How to Restore (Williams)
Triumph Trident T150/T160 & BSA Rocket III, How to Restore (Rooke)
Ultimate Mini Restoration Manual, The (Ayre & Webber)
Volkswagen Beetle, How to Restore (Tyler)
VW Bay Window Bus (Paxton)
Yamaha FS1-E, How to Restore (Watts)

www.veloce.co.uk/www.velocebooks.com

Published in April 2019, reprinted 2024 by Veloce, an imprint of David and Charles Limited. Tel +44 (0)1305 260068 / e-mail info@veloce.co.uk / web www.veloce.co.uk.

ISBN: 978-1-787114-19-7 UPC: 6-36847-01419-3
© 2019 & 2024 Paul Hogan and David and Charles. All rights reserved. With the exception of quoting brief passages for the purpose of review, no part of this publication may be recorded, reproduced or transmitted by any means, including photocopying, without the written permission of David and Charles Limited.

Please do not undertake any of the procedures described in this book unless you feel competent to do so, having first read the full instructions.

Throughout this book logos, model names and designations, etc, have been used for the purposes of identification, illustration and decoration. Such names are the property of the trademark holder as this is not an official publication. Readers with ideas for automotive books, or books on other transport or related hobby subjects, are invited to write to the editorial director of Veloce at the above address. British Library Cataloguing in Publication Data – A catalogue record for this book is available from the British Library. Design and DTP by Veloce. Printed and bound by CPI Group (UK) Ltd, Croydon, CR0 4YY.

Introduction & thanks

Introduction

This guidebook should not be seen as a replacement for the excellent Standard-Triumph workshop manual or its supplements, but rather as an aid for enthusiasts who'd like to know more about the inner workings of the car, how it's put together, and some ideas on how to take it apart!

The TR6 was a development of the previous TR5 (pictured below), which in turn owes its origins to the earlier TR4A. Triumph commissioned the German coachbuilder Karmann to produce a relatively cheap but effective 'facelift' for the TR5, with which Karmann succeeded magnificently.

By retaining most of the internal body structure, doors, windscreen, and interior, Karmann produced a much more modern-looking car, which was very much in tune with the 1970s, but at a fraction of the cost of producing an all-new vehicle.

It would, therefore, be fair to describe the TR6 as a silk purse built on a sow's ear, as underneath that pretty skin is some fairly old technology. The separate chassis and engine date back to the 1950s, but let's not be too hard on Triumph, because through the TR series of sports cars, it introduced a lot of new ideas, which later became common mainstream fitments. Disc brakes, fuel-injection, and face-level ventilation all featured on TRs for the first time in a standard mass-production car.

The first example of the TR6 hit the showrooms in November 1968, and so the earliest cars you will see sport a G registration plate in the UK. They also featured the Rostyle wheel trims as found on the TR5, but these were very soon discontinued in favour of the new standard steel wheel. Wire wheels, of course, were always an option, but fitted with octagonal chrome nuts as opposed to the usual two-eared spinner.

The two-piece 'surrey top,' that featured on the earlier TR4, 4A and 5, was replaced with a more conventional, snug-fitting, fully-glazed steel hardtop, which takes two people to lift on and off the car. Reclining seats were also featured for the first time, but otherwise the interior was virtually the same as the TR5.

Mechanically, the layout also followed the specification for the TR5, with all-round independent suspension; a four-speed gearbox that could be fitted with the optional Laycock de Normanville overdrive operating on 2nd , 3rd , and 4th gears; and a fuel-injected 2.5-litre straight-six engine, reputed to put out a healthy 150bhp, and give a top speed of 120mph.

During its production life, several changes were gradually made in various areas, but the most significant change came in 1973, when the engine was de-tuned to 130bhp, and the overdrive gearbox was changed to the later J-type, operating only on 3rd and 4th gears. Cosmetically, the dashboard received new style instruments and the door cards were modified too. All in all, some 94,619 TR6s were delivered over its eight years of production, with the majority going to America.

In America, which was always Triumph's biggest market for the TR6, the cars were not fitted with fuel-injection, and had to rely on twin Stromberg carburettors in order to meet the strict federal emissions regulations. Other federal safety regulations in 1973 meant large rubber overriders had to be fitted to the front and rear, and the height of the bumpers was raised too, which didn't do much for the looks, but at least they were much better than those fitted to the MGB and Midgets.

As a driver's car, the TR6 was always portrayed as the last of the 'hairy-chested sports cars,' which is possibly another way of saying it was rough and hard to handle; in truth, the car always delivered a good and satisfying ride, and handled reasonably well given its crude underpinnings.

Over the years, many owners have modified their cars, and it's hard to find an original these days. Popular modifications include walnut veneer dashboards and door cappings, fitting more comfortable Mazda MX5 seats and mohair hoods, but it's on the mechanical side that some real performance enhancements can be found: telescopic shock absorber kits can be fitted to replace the lever type at the rear, five-speed gearboxes can replace worn out overdrive units, and throttle bodies can replace the Lucas injection system. Power wise, up to 200bhp can now be obtained from a TR6 engine, which is a big improvement on the 150bhp of the standard unit. Four pot brake callipers can also be fitted to make sure the car can stop as well as it goes.

Buying a car can present the unwary with a multitude of things to look out for, and, of course, there is the ever-present threat of rust and structural failure to take into account. With the youngest of these cars now being over 40 years old, close inspection is advised to anyone thinking of buying one. If you do find a good example, it will be a rewarding car to own, to drive, and, given the state of the classic car market, probably a decent investment too!

Thanks

Very few books are written without some help, and this is no exception. I would like to thank Thomas Boyd and Simon Watson at TR Enterprises in Blidworth, Mansfield, and Darryl Uprichard at Racetorations in Gainsborough, for allowing me to take photographs of a number of cars being worked on in their workshops. I'm also indebted to my good friend Dr Michael Hunter, for providing the picture of a vertical link at short notice. (There's never one lying around when you want one!) My thanks also go to that legendary gentleman and race driver Bob Tullius for his contributions to the book. I would also like to thank my many friends in the TR Register who will no doubt be my worst critics of this work, and in particular I'd like to thank our esteemed Honorary President, Graham Robson – for without his many reference works, my own knowledge of TRs and all things Triumph would be close to nothing.

Contents

Please note: All references to the left or right of the car use the perspective from the driver's seat.

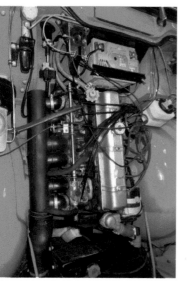

1 Engine

The 2.5 six-cylinder engine fitted to the TR6 is quite a straightforward piece of engineering. It's a cast-iron block fitted with four main bearings, a single duplex chain-driven camshaft operating eight pushrods, topped off with a cast-iron cylinder head with two valves per cylinder.

The sump is a rather basic pressed steel affair that houses the oil pick-up and pump, and the valve cover is also a pressed steel item.

Its design history can be traced back to the Standard Vanguard 'Luxury Six' of 1960, and the basic design powered a variety of Standard-Triumph models, including the Vitesse, GT6, 2000, and 2.5 saloons. During this time, power went up from 80bhp to 150bhp, while the cubic capacity ranged from 1596cc in the Mk1 Vitesse, to 2498cc as used on the TR6 and 2.5 saloons.

The fuel-injection was developed by Lucas and comprised a metering unit fed by a high pressure pump located in the boot.

1.1: The left side of the engine bay.

The metering unit delivered measured amounts of fuel directly into the inlet manifold on the opposite side of the engine. It is fair to say that when fuel-injection (or PI as it was known) was first introduced to the market, many garages didn't have the expertise to set it up correctly, and the reputation of the Lucas PI systems suffered as a result. However, while a properly set up Lucas system is good, it's often let down by the fuel pump, which has a tendency to overheat and cause cavitation. Many owners have retro-fitted Bosch fuel pumps to avoid this problem.

1 Starting

There are a number of problems that can result in a car running rough or not starting, and advice on how to deal with these can be found in the troubleshooting guide of Chapter 21. However, one problem worth looking at in greater detail is the choke – or to give it its proper name, the cold start control.

The TR6 is fitted with a manual choke, which is the control

1.2: The right side of the engine bay.

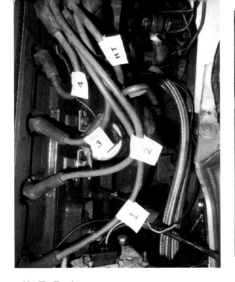

on the right of the centre console. Unlike ordinary chokes, the TR6 has two choke cables: one goes to the metering unit that advances the amount of fuel being delivered to the engine, and the other goes to the manifold linkage. It's important that both of these cables are set up correctly, and even more important to close the choke after starting; with this particular choke, over fuelling the car will result in a very jerky ride. Your instinct may be to increase the amount of choke, but in the case of the TR6, the reverse is true.

The 2.5 engine is a big old lump, and a tired battery will often not produce the amps needed to turn the car over fast enough. More importantly, if there isn't enough current to power up the high pressure fuel pump, then you won't be going anywhere. For this reason alone, it's often very difficult to bump start a TR6. The solution? Check the ammeter to see if there is enough current in the circuit. Another improvement that many owners, including myself, have made, is fitting a high torque starter motor. These really do crank the engine over much faster than one fitted by Triumph, they weigh a lot less than the standard pre-engaged unit, and they have proved very reliable.

2 Low compression

Loss of cylinder head compression is another area to look at. By using a compression tester in the sparkplug holes, you'll be able to tell if you need to remedy this. Making sure that you've disabled the electrical starting circuit by removing the HT leads from the coil/distributor (it's a good idea to put tape on all the HT leads so you can number them one to six), the compression tester should read virtually the same across all six cylinders. If not, and one or more cylinders are markedly down on the readings, you may have head gasket, valve seat, or valve guide problems. Worn cylinder bores, pistons, and piston rings are also indicative of low compression, but they can only be checked by removing the engine and stripping it down.

Low compression can also lead to excessive use of oil, and blue smoke in the exhaust is a good indicator of that. Excess oil getting past the piston rings and into the combustion chambers will mean an engine rebuild is on the cards, and starting will become more difficult as well. You can also check the sparkplugs for signs of oil on them: they should be a good grey colour, not black or wet with oil.

3 Cylinder head gasket

If the head gasket has gone, water vapour (white smoke) in the exhaust is a telltale sign, as is overheating on the temperature gauge, coupled with a loss of coolant. Another indicator of head gasket failure is 'mayonnaise' on the oil filler cap or the dipstick; this is a sure sign that water has got into the oilways of the engine, but before doing anything drastic like removing the head, check that the engine breather pipes are not clogged up.

If it is a case of a head gasket failing, then you will need to remove the cylinder head. This is no easy task as you have to dismantle both the inlet and exhaust manifolds, and remove the injection pipes that run across the top of the engine. Again, it makes sense to number the injectors one to six. Then, you need to remove the top hose from the thermostat housing, so it's a good idea to drain some of the water from the system first by removing the radiator filler cap and using either of the two drain taps fitted – one at the bottom of the radiator, the other on the side of the engine block, underneath the manifold. Remember to refit the radiator cap so as not to lose it.

Once the ancillaries have been cleared away, you can start taking the rocker cover off, to expose the six large cylinder head nuts inside. It's also a good idea to get cylinder number

one to top dead centre. This can be checked by removing the sparkplugs and inserting a thin metal probe – like a screwdriver – into the plug hole. Using the fan, rotate the engine by hand until you feel the piston reach the top of its stroke. When that is done, you can remove the valve gear, making sure that you keep the pushrods in the correct order. Here, a piece of cardboard with holes punched into it, numbered one to 12, will help keep them in the order they came out.

1.5: With the cylinder head removed. Note the alloy plate to protect the cylinder bores.

When all 12 cylinder head nuts have been removed (and sometimes the nut won't come off without the actual stud sometimes coming with it), it should be a straight forward job to lift the head off the block. Invariably, it isn't, as over time the head sticks to the block gasket and the gasket to the block.

Gently tapping the head with a copper hammer often helps to shock release the head, but the key word here is *gently*. It also helps to use the thermostat housing as a 'handle' to assist in lifting the head clear of the block.

Once the head is safely off and on the bench you can inspect the top of the pistons. They should all be consistent in colour, but if water has been seeping into a cylinder then it will look much cleaner than the others.

1.6: Exhaust and inlet valves. Note the different sizes of valves and springs.

The old head gasket should be inspected for breaks between the oil and waterways, and replaced with a new one. Changing a head gasket is a time-consuming exercise so always use a top quality gasket – it's false economy to fit a cheap one.

4 Valves & tuning the head

With the cylinder head on the bench, you can also inspect the combustion chamber, valves, and guides. Valve seats take a lot of hammering, and wear here will be detrimental to the health of the engine; if the valves seem okay then it shouldn't need much more than a decoke. However, if you want to extract more power from the engine then now is the time to do it. Send the head to a *reputable* workshop, one experienced in working such heads. Insist that new phosphor bronze valve guides are fitted, then match and gas flow the inlet and exhaust ports to whatever manifolds are to be used. Also, if they haven't already been done previously, the valve seats themselves will need to be replaced with hardened versions in order to work with unleaded fuel. This is another job the engine specialist can carry out for you.

5 Oil, lubrication & cooling

I think it's fair to say that virtually all Triumph engines leak a bit of oil, and the TR6's 2.5 lump is no exception. The good news is, if you do have a leaky engine, you will be topping it up every 800-1000 miles with fresh, clean oil, and what escapes will do a good job of helping to preserve the chassis!

When starting from cold, the oil in the engine will be thicker, but it has to do its lubrication job immediately, otherwise the engine could seize up. Much has been written about the use of modern versus traditional oil in these types of engines, and the accepted wisdom is that you can't really go wrong with a 20w/50 multigrade oil. However, if you are only using your TR6 during the summer months then why use winter grade oil at all? Straight SAE 50 will do the job just as well and should be a bit cheaper to buy.

1.7: The oil pump stripped bare. Note the eccentric rotor.

1.8: The original type oil filter, sealing ring and canister.

5.1 The oil pump

The oil pump is driven by a skew gear on the camshaft, which is also connected to the distributor drive spindle. The pump is a fairly simple affair, and consists of a pick-up nozzle and eccentric rotor, housed in the pump body. Being virtually immersed in oil, they are very reliable units and rarely fail. For competition work, it is possible to fit an up-rated oil pump, which produces a greater flow of oil, but on a standard road car this is unnecessary.

5.2 The oil filter

As mentioned above, the standard oil filter is housed in a canister just below the distributor drive column. It's located by a central spindle and care should be taken when removing the canister, so be ready with a container to catch the old oil which is guaranteed to pour out of it!

1.9: A 'spin on' oil filter and adaptor plate.

1.10: A 13-row oil cooler fitted with steel braided hoses.

1.11: An oil thermostat on this TR6 has been fitted to the pipes leading to the oil cooler.

The filter itself comprises the paper element, a large domed washer, a tensioning spring, and two small washers. It's important to check that the small washers do not get thrown away with the old filter. The new filter should come with a larger rubber sealing ring. This sits in the locating groove machined into the block. Remember to remove the old sealing ring first – which can be done with a small flat-bladed screwdriver – and then carefully fit the new sealing ring. Reassemble the canister with the spring, the small washers, and the large domed washer in the correct order, and slide the new filter element into the canister. The large domed washer acts as a spring-loaded plate that keeps the oil filter element in the correct position. Failure to place these parts in the correct order will enable unfiltered oil to pass back into the engine, so do take care when reassembling. Carefully put the spindle into the block and bolt it into position. WARNING: Do *not* attempt to over-tighten the spindle as excessive force can crack the cast-iron housing it screws into, with disastrous results.

When all is in place, top up with fresh, clean oil as necessary and check for leaks. If there is a leak from the canister, the large sealing ring is probably not properly seated in its groove.

One alternative to the standard filter arrangement is to convert to a 'spin off' canister system. The standard can and separate element are replaced with an alloy adaptor plate and a screw-on filter. It certainly makes an oil change a much less messy affair, and the parts are readily available from most TR specialist suppliers.

6 Oil pressure relief valve

The pressure relief valve is located on the left-hand side of the engine block, just in front of the oil filter. It can be easily identified by its octagonal shape, and removed with the aid of a suitably-sized spanner or socket.

The valve itself is a spring-loaded ball, and care should be

taken to see that no grit or other particles contaminate the housing or the parts. TRs are quite good when it comes to oil pressure, and a general rule of thumb is that oil pressure should be at least 40psi at 2000rpm when hot. Any lower than this and it's a sign of wear inside the engine. Under normal running conditions, it's not unusual to see oil pressure in the 70psi region. If oil pressure is running low, it can be tempting to alter the pressure rate on the relief valve by changing the length of the spring, but the author strongly advises against doing so. It's better to trace the fault and replace any parts that need attention instead.

Low oil pressure will obviously affect the way oil is pumped around the engine, and too little oil being sent to the bearings will rapidly increase engine wear. Conversely, too high an oil pressure can also affect an engine's performance: if it sounds like the engine is knocking or making other rumbling sounds, then it may be due to the pressure relief valve being tampered with in order to get the oil pressure gauge to give a higher reading.

7 Oil coolers

Another topic that often crops up among owners is whether or not to fit an oil cooler. There are a number of oil cooler kits on the market, and they are very good, too. The best ones use an adaptor plate which allows you to use a 'spin on' oil filter instead of the standard canister: much cleaner and less messy. The cooler is usually a 13-row type, and most owners fit it in front of the water radiator where there is a convenient gap in the front apron of the car.

Ideally, the oil radiator should be as close to the water radiator as it can be, but it's possible to bolt it to the top of the sumpguard where it will work just as well. *But*, is it actually necessary? If the car gets driven hard or used in competition work, the answer is yes. On a car that is only used on weekends? Probably not.

Research by some oil companies has concluded that oil rarely ever gets up to a temperature whereby it will start to break down, and most cars never even get their oil hot enough to do the job it is designed to do. It's therefore recommended that if you do fit an oil cooler, an oil stat should also be plumbed into the pipe work.

8 Oil change intervals

The driver's handbook recommends oil changes every 6000 miles, but many classic cars today never cover that many miles in a year. Therefore, if the car is only being used for six months of the year, or during the summer months, then changing the oil and filter around March/April should be sufficient. If the car is to be laid up for a long period of time in secure storage, then it is recommended to remove the sparkplugs and spray the cylinders with clean engine oil in order to stop the bores rusting. However, if you do follow this advice, do *not* attempt to start the car before draining off any excess oil, otherwise serious damage to the engine can occur.

2 Unusual engine noises

Today, we are accustomed to driving cars that are quiet and emit very little engine noise. However, the TR6 was designed in another era, when engine noise was not only to be expected, but often welcomed as a sign of a powerful car. Rattles, though, are a different matter, and it's fair to say that the TR6 can experience its fair share of them.

1 Valve train noise

Starting at the top of the engine, the biggest source of noise will come from the valve gear. Rattles here are a sign of incorrectly set valve clearances, a worn rocker shaft, or worn tappets. Valve clearances should only be set when the engine is cold. Cars fitted with higher lift cams and heavy-duty valve springs can be expected to generate slightly more noise, but it shouldn't be excessive. If it is excessive, then there may be another problem.

2 Timing chain rattle

Timing chain rattle is probably the easiest noise to identify, but isn't necessarily the easiest to fix. The TR6 is fitted with a duplex timing chain for strength, and directs power to the camshaft from the crankshaft. It's tensioned by a flat spring steel blade, and this is often the cause of noise from this source. If the tensioner is badly worn, the blades of the spring can actually break at the point where the tensioner is fitted into the timing chest. The blade is held in place by a washer and a circlip, and is an easy part to replace once the timing chest cover has been removed.

Replacing the chain itself is not so easy, as it calls for removal of the crank pulley. However, once access is gained, the timing chest cover can be removed quite easily, the locking bolts that secure the timing gears can be undone, and the duplex chain removed. Great care must be taken not to disturb the engine

2.1: Numbered pushrods and valve gear.

2.2: The duplex timing chain assembly. Note the single row timing gears on the right that were fitted to some engines.

timing, and it is advisable to use some Tippex to mark the positions on the gears. It's also advisable to closely inspect the timing gears: replacing a worn chain and tensioner won't cure the problem if the timing gear teeth are also badly worn.

2.3: One half of a crank thrust washer.

2.4: Pinning the top half of this rear thrust washer with brass pins stops it rotating and wearing away.

3 Crank thrust washers

Wear and tear is part and parcel of every engine's life, and the TR6 is no different. One of the most common areas of wear is on the crankshaft thrust washers, which shows up as crankshaft end float. Low oil pressure is one of first things you might notice due to worn thrust washers, but you can diagnose this by getting someone to press the clutch pedal while you look at the crank pulley mounted on the front of the engine. If you see it move, you can bet your life that the rear thrust washer is worn – the best way to fix this is to take the engine out.

TR6 rear thrust washers are a two-piece affair, and can wear very quickly, ruining the rear crank face if not replaced in time. They are available in oversized sizes, and its recommended that at least one of the washers halves are drilled to take small pins, sometimes known as roll pins, to stop them rotating with the crank. (The author did this modification many years ago on the lower main bearing cap and it does work.)

4 Crank shaft bearings

If you think your TR6 is starting to sound like a diesel engine, you have a problem! The problem will almost certainly be worn big end bearings, either on the con rods, or on the four main crankshaft bearings, or probably both. The noise will be most evident on start-up from cold, or when the oil is really hot and thinner. The oil pressure gauge will provide a visual clue as to the state of the engine – anything below 20psi is going to be pretty serious.

There are no quick fixes for this; it'll be an engine out job, and a proper bottom end rebuild. While it is possible to just replace the affected bearing shells, it is a false economy to do so. With the engine out of the car and stripped down, now is the perfect time to undertake a proper rebuild in order to make sure the car will be fit for the next 100,000 miles.

2.5: On the left is a standard piston and con rod. A competition version with a forged piston and a much stronger 'H' beam rod is on the right.

5 Pinking

This is the sound associated with petrol cars that have their ignition timing out. Usually, it is because the ignition is too far advanced, and so the fuel has a tendency to 'explode' in the combustion chamber, rather than 'burn' as it should. Very high temperatures are generated, and this can lead to valves and pistons burning. Other causes of pinking include using fuel with too low an octane rating, a very weak fuel mixture, and an engine that needs a decoke. The fuel-injected TR6 was designed to run on five-star fuels, but as they are almost impossible to come by these days, the cars will quite happily run on four-star fuels, as long as the timing is adjusted accordingly.

6 Piston slap

Piston slap can occur when an engine is cold, and before it has had a chance to work up to its operating temperature. Often, it's a sign of worn pistons, or more likely the piston rings themselves. It can also manifest with high oil consumption. If the noise disappears when the engine gets hot, it's not something you should worry about, but if it persists and oil consumption is noticeably higher, an engine rebuild is on the cards.

7 Drivebelt screech

If your car sounds like a banshee on start-up, it's a sure sign of a badly slipping/adjusted fan belt. One thing that's worth checking is the alignment of the pulleys, especially that of the alternator: they should be in line with each other. When replacing a fan belt,

do not be tempted to over tighten it. Another similar source of noise in this area can be the water pump bearing announcing that it's about to fail and needs replacing ASAP.

8 Chuffing & sputtering

TR6s are renowned for sputtering when starting up in the morning from cold. Once they are warmed up, they should perform really well, with only the deep thrum from the exhaust. If the engine continues to cough and splutter, there may be a problem with the head gasket, or more likely with the exhaust gaskets. It is also worth checking the condition of any pipe work attached to the inlet manifold for cracks and leaks, as this, too, can cause spluttering if the fuel-air mixture is wrong.

1 The gearbox, overdrive & clutch

The TR6 gearbox is a hefty piece of kit, and was available in overdrive and non-overdrive versions. For some reason not known to the author, it seems the majority of cars sold in the USA were not fitted with overdrive, but if you are considering importing a TR6 from the States, it is relatively straightforward, albeit expensive, to convert a non-overdrive gearbox into an overdrive one.

Both types of gearbox offer four forward gears and one reverse. The ratios are reasonably well placed to provide adequate acceleration through the gears and a decent cruising speed.

There were two types of overdrive unit offered during the TR6's production run: the A-type and the later J-type (see photo 3.2). The A-type offers three further ratios on 2nd, 3rd, and 4th gears, while the J-type only worked on 3rd and 4th. As a general rule, these J-type units are found on de-tuned 135bhp versions of the

3.1: The four-speed gearbox fitted with an A-type overdrive unit.

TR6, but so many conversions have taken place over the years, it's not possible to use that as a reliable guide for working out which model you have. Cars that were fitted with an overdrive at the factory have a letter O stamped on the commission plate – for example, CF57235-O.

Generally, the gearbox in all its guises is a pretty robust unit, but they do suffer from synchromesh gear wear, and the main shaft bearings can also wear pretty badly. The top cover holds the selector forks, as well as the isolator switches for the overdrive and the reversing light switch.

2 Removing the gearbox

Extracting the gearbox from the car can be done by anyone competent with a spanner, but it can be a struggle. A lift or a pit makes the job so much easier. The gearbox is removed from inside the car, so you will need to remove both seats from their runners, the carpets, and the H piece that holds the radio. When that is all cleared away, disconnect the electrical feed for the overdrive and reversing lights, and unbolt the gearbox cover. It helps if the handbrake lever is also disconnected. With the gearbox cover removed, you can now access the bolts that hold the gearbox in place.

Start by disconnecting the speedo cable drive from the gearbox, then undo the four propshaft bolts, noting which way round they are (see photo 9.1). The rear gearbox mounting bolts can then be undone, and, if fitted, the gearbox exhaust bracket as well. Several of the bolts that hold the bell housing to the engine can also be undone from inside the car, but others need to be accessed from underneath, or from inside the engine bay.

While underneath the car, disconnect the clutch release arm from the clutch slave cylinder, and remove the bracket holding it to the bell housing. Also, don't forget to remove the engine earth strap from the bulkhead and gearbox. The starter motor also needs to be unbolted, and, if possible, removed from the gearbox.

3.2: A two-piece gearbox cover aids access.

3.3: The speedo angle drive.

With all the bolts removed from the bell housing, and the engine suitably supported – either from under the sump or from an engine crane – the gearbox can now be extracted from inside the car. Remember, it is VERY HEAVY and may need two people to pull it out of the car. It's not unknown for the release bearing to fall off when doing this, but by wiring the arm to the bell housing, it is possible to keep it in place.

It is not within the scope of this book to explain how to dismantle the gearbox. My recommendation is to take it to a specialist who can strip it down and check for wear, and, if needs be, recondition it, or even uprate it by fitting the stronger STAG bearings and main shaft. The overdrive unit can also be uprated to 28% pressure.

3 The overdrive

Overdrives were common fitments to many cars in the 1950s and '60s, but have since been replaced by five-speed gearboxes. Built by Laycock de Normanville, the TR range had overdrives from the very beginning, the TR6 being no exception. They allow easy high-speed cruising at low revs, and trickling along in traffic without revving the engine. However, they are also prone to malfunction!

The overdrive is operated by a lever on the steering column, although some cars fitted with a STAG gearbox can have this switch on the gear lever. It's a compound system using an electrical circuit to operate a solenoid, which in turn activates the hydraulic pump inside the overdrive. With several electrical connections in the overdrive wiring circuit, fault finding can be frustrating. Start by checking the operation of the solenoid first, and see that the control lever moves correctly. If it doesn't move, you have a fault in the electrical circuit. If it does, but doesn't operate the overdrive, it may be a simple question of adjustment. The small hole at the end of the lever should line up with another

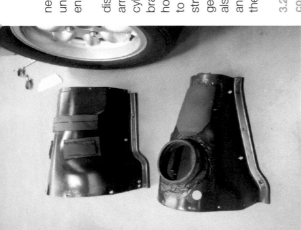

small hole in the overdrive casing. You can use a ⅛in diameter drill to check this. If it's still not working, you may need to take the gearbox out of the car to fix it.

Both types of overdrive require oil to operate properly, and a low gearbox oil level will not help things. However, the owner

3.4: The smaller J-type overdrive unit.

3.5: Topping up the gearbox oil.

handbook specifies the use of EP90 gear oil, while the Laycock manual specifically says to NOT use Extreme Pressure oil in an overdrive gearbox. The author has always followed the Laycock advice, and used SAE30 gear oil with no problems in 40 years of TR ownership.

4 The clutch cover & plate

With the gearbox out of the way, attention can now be turned to the clutch. The TR6 uses either a Laycock or Borg and Beck dry plate type clutch and spring diaphragm clutch cover. It's bolted to the flywheel and kept in position by studs. Removing the clutch cover is simple, but you may need to 'chock' the engine (to stop it turning while undoing the bolts) by jamming the starter ring on the flywheel. With the cover out of the way, the clutch plate can be removed for inspection. My general advice is to replace both the clutch plate and cover with new ones, unless they have recently been replaced already and are showing no signs of wear. The same can be said for the release bearing, too.

3.6: The clutch release bearing and cross shaft.

5 The clutch release bearing

The release bearing does exactly what it says. Pressure on the clutch pedal pushes the bearing forward onto the springs of the clutch cover to enable gear changes. The bearing can rattle, and has even been known to come off its forked carrier due to wear. Check for rattles and replace if required.

6 Operating problems

The clutch is hydraulically operated via a slave cylinder mounted on the bell housing, and this may be the first port of call for investigating clutch problems. Symptoms of clutch failure can be indicated by difficulty in engaging gear, or by a noticeably lighter clutch pedal. Both the slave master cylinders can leak, so it's best to check the fluid levels first. Also check for signs of leaking by peeling back the dust covers on each cylinder. Both seals can be easily replaced, but if the bores are worn, the only real fix is to replace the damaged cylinder; it is preferable to replace both at the same time.

7 Clutch judder

A worn or contaminated clutch will sometimes manifest itself by juddering as it tries to take up the drive. Sometimes, it's caused by oil contamination from a leaking seal in the gearbox, or from the rear crank oil seal. Another possible cause is from badly worn engine and gearbox rubber mountings.

8 The spigot bearing

With the flywheel now exposed, it's possible – and advisable – to check the condition of the phosphor bronze spigot bearing in the end of the crankshaft. To do this, remove the flywheel from the crank by undoing the bolts holding the two together. With the end of the crank now exposed, you can extract the spigot bush from

the crank. If it's showing signs of wear, a quick fix is to simply turn it around and refit it, but if you can get a new one then so much the better.

9 Gear change problems

A badly worn gearbox will make the car difficult to drive. Gears will crunch, jump out, and selection will be difficult. Do not attempt to hide this by putting thicker oil in the gearbox, as some unscrupulous owners might try to do. A gearbox rebuild is the only sensible option. However, one minor irritation may be caused by the gearlever itself rattling, and this can be cured simply, by fitting a new anti-rattle spring in the base of the lever.

10 Competition options

Apart from upgrading to STAG internals, anyone contemplating competition could fit close ratio gear clusters, and/or a hydraulic release bearing. The overdrive operating switch can also be fitted to the gearlever if so desired. For out-and-out racing, a dog box can be specified, but these are not recommended for any road use: they are incredibly noisy and gear changing can be difficult.

3.7: The clutch master reservoir.

4 Fuel & exhaust systems

Potential new owners of TR6s have a choice to make: do you stick to the original fuel-injection setup – which means buying a UK-registered car with all of its attendant rust problems – or do you import a 'rust-free' LHD conversion with carburettors, as fitted to US export cars? A purist would no doubt prefer the original injection system, but that was designed to run on leaded 100 octane fuel – or five-star as it was known back then. However, leaded five-star hasn't been available for many years now, so all TRs have to run on 98 octane unleaded fuel – it's a bit of a Hobson's choice, really. You could, of course, opt to put an additive or octane booster product in your tank, but as long as the valve seats have been replaced with hardened ones, I have never had to resort to using such products.

4.1: The steel fuel tank.

1 Fuel tank & filler

The fuel tank on the TR6 is a pressed steel affair, located between the cockpit and the boot. The tank holds approximately 11 imperial gallons (50 litres) of fuel, and with typical fuel consumption of 19-22mpg, it gives the car a useable range of about 250 miles. However, some aftermarket reproduction tanks can offer a capacity of up to 14 gallons (64 litres), and are available in either aluminium or stainless steel construction.

Essentially, there are two types of fuel tank: one fitted to the fuel-injected cars, and one for cars fitted with carburettors. Both tanks share the common inlet at the top of the tank, due to the centrally placed fuel filler on the rear deck or saddle of the car. The filler cap itself can also be indicative of where the car originated from, as at least two different designs were used.

The fuel-injected versions need a return feed to send excess petrol back to the tank from the metering unit, whereas the normally-aspirated cars do not. A brass return fitting located in the top of the tank would quickly help to identify whether the tank was for a PI car or not. Both tanks also feature breathers on the filler caps and the tanks themselves. However, for emission control, USA spec cars had a sealed fuel cap.

The fuel gauge sender is located in the top face of the tank, and is generally a very reliable unit. Floats have been known to spring a leak, however, but it is a straight-forward job to replace the sender unit. The fuel gauge itself is also very reliable in service, but it is unwise to allow the fuel in the tank to fall near empty. Despite the presence of in-line filters, dirt, debris, and rust can build up in a tank and cause blockages to the system.

It's better to keep the tank topped up if possible, although if the car is being kept in storage for long periods of time, it's better to drain the system, as the fuel will lose its volatility over time and invite water contamination from condensation.

However, steel tanks suffer from internal corrosion, as fuel always has some water in it, and an empty tank will also be exposed to water vapour. Usually, the corrosion isn't serious, but sediment and flaking can build up in the tank and clog the outlets. If that's the case, it's maybe time to consider fitting an aluminium tank instead. Not cheap, but it's a fit-and-forget option.

2 Cars exported to America

Later cars that were exported to the USA have a slightly smaller fuel tank capacity compared to the early ones, because Triumph fitted larger cross section tyres, and needed a bit more space in the boot to accommodate the spare wheel.

3 Fuel-injected cars

Located below the fuel tank, on the left-hand side of the car, is a CAV-type fuel filter. This is often neglected, and should be replaced in accordance with the manufacturer's service requirement. Also check for water contamination if the car has been left standing for long periods without being regularly turned over. From the CAV filter, fuel feeds the Lucas high pressure pump, which in turn feeds the engine's metering unit. I know from experience how hot this pump can get, and both the TR5 and the TR6 can suffer from cavitation in the pump. Lucas did produce a cooling coil that fitted over the body of the pump and was fed by the petrol return from the engine, but its efficacy was always suspect.

4.3: The CAV fuel filter is located in the spare wheel tray.

4.2: A replacement alloy fuel tank. It's much lighter, and no rust.

If overheating does occur, a quick remedy is to get a packet of frozen peas and place it against the pump body – if this sounds like an urban myth, I can assure you it is not! Other remedies that owners have used to help cool the pump are: cutting a hole in the inner wing to let hot air out; fitting a scoop under the boot floor to force cooler air into boot; and fitting a small cooling fan from a laptop to blow air over the pump. How effective any of these measures are is hard to tell, but having tried the frozen peas method myself, I know it works!

One other problem with the pump, which owners should be aware of, is that it requires a fully-charged battery. As a high pressure pump, it draws a lot more current than a standard SU pump, so if the battery is not fully charged, the starting circuit just won't have enough power to turn the engine over and deliver fuel to it. However, when the ignition is turned on, you will hear the pump give a high-pitched whine. If it sounds slow and sluggish, you have a

4.4: The Lucas fuel pump.

problem. If it's not the battery, it will be more serious and the fault will lie in the pump itself.

The main fuel pipes run down the inside of the left-hand chassis members to where a pressure relief valve can be found.

4.5: The Lucas metering unit.

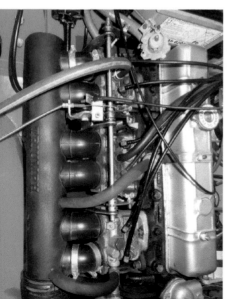

4.6: Note the six thin black pipes feeding the injectors in the inlet manifold.

From here, the pipes continue forward to the engine bay and the metering unit. The large braided hose going up to the metering unit is the inlet pipe, and the smaller section pipe is the one that goes back to the tank.

4 The metering unit

The Lucas system employs a mechanical metering unit, which delivers fuel to the inlet manifold via high pressure injectors. It's located on the left-hand side of the engine, just above the oil filter; the best advice for the home mechanic is to leave it well alone! A spring-loaded shuttle helps to deliver what should be the right amount of fuel to the engine, but unless you have access to some very good kit, any problems with the unit are best left for a specialist to sort out.

If the engine does seem to be running rough, it is possible to check that fuel is being delivered to the manifold correctly. It's also possible to feel the 'pulses' of fuel being fed to the injectors, and by removing an injector, you'll be able to see if the spray

pattern is a consistent cone shape. If it isn't, or if it dribbles fuel, then a sticking injector may be the cause, and it will need to be replaced.

5 Cars fitted with Bosch fuel pumps

Both the TR5 and TR6 gained a reputation for poor running, due to badly set up Lucas systems and ignorance on the part of the general garage trade, who had never come across fuel-injection before. One should remember that the TR5 was the first mass-produced sports car to be fitted with PI, as up until then, only Ferraris and the like used it – and how often does one of those end up in the hands of a local garage?

One aftermarket solution was to fit a Bosch fuel pump. These conversions are generally regarded as being more reliable than the factory-fitted pump, but they do not come cheap. However, it has to be said that a properly set up Lucas system works just fine. More often than not, problems only arise when poor maintenance has been carried out.

4.7: A Bosch fuel pump conversion.

4.8: This USA spec car shows its original Stromberg carburettors.

6 Cars fitted with carburettors

Due to more stringent emission regulations, fuel-injected cars were never offered for sale in the USA. The former TR5 was badged in the US as a TR250, and was fitted with two 1¾in Stromberg 175CD carburettors, and the US spec TR6 used the same setup. Incidentally, TR6s were never fitted with SU carbs by the factory, so any car fitted with SUs has been modified later on by an enthusiast. One such conversion uses a new inlet manifold to take three 1¾in SU carbs, while another more popular modification is to fit three Weber DCOE 40/45 carburettors.

If money is no object, and if even more power is required, some tuning shops now offer a modern take on the old fuel-injection system, by selling a kit for a TR6 with a fully-mapped engine management system with direct injection via throttle bodies.

Perhaps the one advantage of not having a PI system is that you don't require the high pressure fuel pump. An SU or Facet Red Top electric fuel pump is often used, and these do tend to be more reliable than the Lucas item, as they are not so prone

4.9: A tubular exhaust manifold.

to overheating. However, like every mechanical device, the electric pump has its own shortcomings. Pumps can fail due to contamination, a broken non return valve or pump diaphragm, or even worn electrical contacts. A good healthy pump will not leak, and can be heard clicking away happily in the boot – or, in some cases, under the bonnet – when the ignition is first turned on.

7 The exhaust system

The standard exhaust system on the TR6 is a straightforward affair, consisting of the exhaust manifold, twin down pipes, forward and rear intermediate pipes, and the transverse silencer box. The original pipe work is made of mild steel, and, of course, rusts. A lot of cars have now had this mild steel system replaced with a stainless steel version, either to the original pattern, or with twin silencer boxes. A tubular exhaust manifold is also often fitted to replace the cast-iron one.

Starting from the engine, you will find the cast-iron exhaust manifold that feeds the six outlets into two down pipes. The iron manifold has been known to crack, which can cause the engine to run rough. A gasket which combines the inlet and exhaust ports is used to seal the manifolds to the block, and is held in place by brass nuts and locating lugs.

The twin mild steel down pipes are fixed to the iron manifold by four studs and a gasket, and can be difficult to remove, as they have a tendency to shear off. If that happens, it's best to remove the manifold itself, in order to get at the offending stud. Of course, in order to do that, the inlet manifold and its associated fittings also have to be removed.

The intermediate pipes have a bracket that secures them to the rear gearbox mounting, and they then pass through the chassis box section, back towards the silencer box. Being close to the road, the silencer box often gets hit by speed bumps and the like.

8 Emissions

The UK TR6 never really had to worry about emissions testing when new, and even today, when taking your car for an MOT, it doesn't fall foul of the exhaust gas analyser regulations. However, in the USA, things were very different, and in California, which was a prime marketplace for British sports cars of that era, the emission lobby drafted some tough laws which a fuel-injected TR6 just couldn't abide by.

US emissions regulations were drawn up in order to prevent any fluids or fuel vapour from venting directly into the atmosphere. The system employed on the TR6 passed contaminated air back into the fuel tank via a vapour separator located on top of the fuel tank, and it also required the fuel filler on the tank to be sealed as well. In addition, an Air-Injection System (AIS) and an Exhaust Gas Recirculation system (EGR) were also added to US spec TR6s in an effort to reduce the amount of hydrocarbon and carbon monoxide produced in the exhaust. This was achieved via a belt-driven air pump, located on the front left-hand side of the engine, just above the alternator.

The effect of these regulations 'strangled' the power output of the 2.5 engine to not much more than that of the previous generation – the TR4 – with its 2.2-litre four-cylinder engine. Nevertheless, the TR6 remained a popular car in the USA.

Some UK and European owners of imported TR6s have been known to remove all of the American spec emissions gear, and replace it with modern fuel-injection systems or triple Weber carburettors as shown in 4.10.

4.10: A much-modified TR6 with a triple Weber carburettor setup.

Check for dents and scouring on the bottom of the silencer. The rear mounting bracket can also come adrift from the chassis due to rust, or from a perished fabric strap. Replace as necessary.

If the original cast-iron manifold is replaced with a stainless steel tubular one, it is advisable to fit some form of heat shield between it and the inlet manifold; this is even more important if carburettors are fitted, as the extra heat generated can cause fuel vaporisation, with its attendant rough running. Wrapping the new manifold in heat insulating fabric is one method, a ceramic coating like Zircotec being a more expensive option.

5 The ignition system

All TR6s were fitted with Lucas ignition systems comprising a standard HT coil, a type 22D6 distributor fitted with contact breaker points, and a condenser. The distributor also operates the rev counter drive. However, those fitted to fuel-injected engines differ from the American spec ones fitted with carburettors. Identification numbers are stamped into the distributor body and this should be referred to, as it is not unknown for a car to have been rebuilt using the wrong type of distributor.

5.1: The alternator, coil and distributor.

1 Common problems

Unseen wear is probably the biggest problem facing TR6 owners today. Not only is it hard to see, it can also be difficult to trace. Both the low tension (LT) and high tension (HT) sides of the ignition circuitry can cause problems, and these usually manifest themselves when trying to start the car. They can, however, also bring a vehicle to an unexpected halt, with no immediately visible signs of a problem.

Wear is also compounded by the dubious quality of some remanufactured parts, especially on the rotor arm and distributor (dizzy) cap, which have been known to fail in operation. Finally, check the condition of ALL the wiring. Very often a fault can be traced to a cracked or broken wire in the HT or LT circuits, and it's much cheaper to replace a set of plug leads than to have a dizzy rebuilt.

2 The distributor

Although a relatively small part of TR6 mechanicals, the distributor is one of the most important components of the engine, and it needs to be looked after.

High mileage cars will suffer from wear on the main drive shaft of the distributor and its bearings. If you can feel any lateral play in the shaft, a rebuild by a specialist will be required. Any play here means the car will suffer from an inconsistent contact breaker gap and dwell angle, and make setting the points accurately impossible.

5.3: Check you have the right sparkplug and it is correctly gapped.

5.2: The rotor arm, capacitor and contact breaker.

Fluctuations in voltage and ignition timing may also be experienced.

The distributor cap can also suffer hairline cracks, and both the central spring-loaded HT carbon contact, and the individual plug lead contacts can show signs of wear. If in doubt, replace it, especially if you experience difficulty with starting in damp weather.

Other key parts located inside the distributor are a small capacitor, the base plate, the points, and, of course, the rotor arm. The base plate can become loose and move inside the distributor, which will make it very difficult to adjust the points. The points themselves can burn, and the pivot should be lubricated with a drop of light grade, 3-in-1 type oil at the same time as the dizzy shaft is given a small amount of grease.

3 The sparkplugs

When having trouble starting an engine, one of the first things to check is the condition of the sparkplugs. Dirty, oil or petrol-soaked plugs will not help starting, so make sure they are clean, dry and properly gapped. 0.015thou is the normal gap, and in the absence of a feeler gauge, one trick often used by mechanics is to tear up a cigarette packet to use as an impromptu gauge. Also, make sure the correct sparkplug has been fitted. It might sound obvious, but also check the white insulator on the plugs for cracks, and do not over tighten them.

When checking the plugs, make sure the number printed on them matches that in the handbook. They should be Champion N-9Y, but if not, the engine may have been modified in some way which required 'hotter' plugs. The colour of the plugs' electrodes is also a good indicator of the health of the engine. Every plug should be the same grey colour, but if one or two are significantly different, that, too, could be a good indicator of wear in that

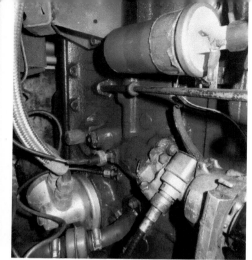

5.4: An up-rated 'gold' coil gives better performance.

5.5: This TR6 has had its distributor replaced with an EI control pack.

particular combustion chamber. Replace the plugs with new ones, and if it still persists, further diagnosis will be required to find the cause of the problem, possibly loss of compression or piston ring wear.

4 The coil

The coil forms part of the high tension (HT) circuit, and is bolted to the side of the engine. They do get hot and this can cause them to fail; some owners prefer to relocate them to the wheelarch, or even fit a spare coil alongside it.

Other problems can be caused by loose spade connectors or a broken wire due to age, vibration, or even corrosion. If the engine cuts out when hot, then the coil itself may be at fault. Let the engine cool down, and if it restarts, it's almost certainly the coil that is faulty. Replace it with a sports coil if possible.

5 Electronic ignition

Often viewed as a 'magic cure' for old ignition systems, the fitting of solid state electronic ignition (EI) has become a very popular modification because of its 'fit-and-forget' advertising slogans. EI is undoubtedly very reliable, and performs well under most conditions.

Early systems required a separate black box to be mounted externally to the engine, but today it is possible to have an EI distributor fitted, while keeping the engine bay looking completely original. The author has tried both systems, and has found very little difference between the two in every day running, but still carries a spare set of points in his travelling tool kit.

6 Starting problems

Poor starting can be traced to a number of problems, but after eliminating the most obvious cause – having no petrol! – the next thing to check is whether there's a spark. Removing a plug lead and shorting it to earth on the rocker cover will reveal if there is a spark – if there is a good spark then the problem will probably lie elsewhere. Alternatively, remove a sparkplug and see if there is a good spark there.

If there is no spark, or only a very weak one, the problem is likely to be in either the HT or LT circuits. A multimeter check on the ignition circuit should show a reading of 12V on the input coil. If not, check your battery is giving you the full 12 volts required. Often when cars have been left standing over the winter, the battery is one of the first things to give up. Using a low voltage trickle charger can help prevent this.

Next, remove the distributor cap and check you have a spark at the points, and that the contacts are in good condition. Again, if there is no spark, it might be a broken wire on the LT side of the distributor. Also check the distributor and rotor arm for cracks and wear. Finally, don't forget to check the seven HT leads as they, too, can deteriorate over time.

7 Running-on problems

If the engine continues to run for a short time after the ignition has been turned off, there is a problem with the fuel/air mixture, which is causing the fuel vapour to detonate due to excessive heat in the combustion chamber, rather than by the sparkplug itself.

Possible causes of this are over-advanced ignition timing, too high an idling speed (it should be 750-800rpm, not 1000rpm), a very high compression ratio, or an excess of carbon build-up in the combustion chamber creating hot spots. If none of these issues is present, it might be necessary to fit an aftermarket anti run-on valve, which would allow more air to enter the engine.

6 The cooling system

The TR6 uses a vertical flow radiator with a standard 15lb/in² pressure cap. A fixed, multi-blade, engine-driven fan is mounted on the crankshaft pulley to provide a cooling draft, and a radiator shroud is fitted to channel outside air through the radiator and into the air filter canister. The thermostat housing – situated at the front of the engine – controls the operating temperature, and water is circulated by a four-bladed, belt-driven water pump. There is also a self-siphoning overflow/expansion bottle fitted on the left-hand side wheelarch.

1 Coolant leaks

Any loss of coolant should be immediately apparent from the temperature gauge, and should be investigated straight away. Leaks from hoses, or the radiator itself, should be easy to spot. Less obvious are leaks from core plugs in the block (of which there are several), or from the heater circuit, which can sometimes be identified by windscreen misting. The water pump, too, can give problems if the bearing starts to fail. Rusty coolant water stains are often the best telltale way to trace a leak, and for the most part, rectification is a straight forward replacement of the affected parts.

If, however, white smoke is seen coming from the exhaust, and your coolant constantly needs topping up, then head gasket failure is the most likely cause.

2 Overheating

The temperature gauge should be holding at a steady 70 degrees, but on long hills it is quite normal for the needle to climb to 80 – or even more – though it should quickly return to

normal afterwards. If it persists in reading higher temperatures, it's indicative of a cooling system deficiency. This may be due to poor water circulation, a blocked radiator, a sticking thermostat, low coolant level, and the aforementioned cylinder head gasket failure.

Under normal driving conditions, most cars never need a fan, as enough air is pushed through the radiator. It's only in town driving or in a queue of traffic that the fan comes into its own. Many owners dispense with the original fan and fit an electric one instead, complete with a manual override in the cockpit. If going down this route, it is important to not only fit the correct fan, but

6.1: This TR6 has been fitted with an alloy radiator, an electric fan and a non-standard radiator cowling.

to make sure it's the right way round! Experience says it's best to fit a new fan behind, and as close to the radiator as possible, rather than in front of it.

After many miles on the road, the radiator can also become blocked with a build-up of debris and insects. The best way to cure this is to remove the radiator, and use a high pressure hose to clean it.

Another source of overheating can be from inside the engine block itself. Over the years, the build up of sediment in the water jacket of the iron block can severely restrict water flow around the engine. The author has, in the past, even found casting sand still in situ when undertaking an engine rebuild. Sediment can be removed with propriety flushing compounds, but it might be necessary to remove the core plugs to remove all the deposits. Finally, owners should be aware that any rally plates, spotlights, or badges fixed in front of the grille can also decrease the cooling power of your car.

6.2: Old and new thermostats. The one on the left is shown in the open position.

3 Overcooling

It is rare to find a car that is overcooled, or fails to reach a normal operating temperature, but it can happen. Usually, it's nothing more than a broken sender unit from the thermostat housing, but it might also be the gauge itself which is at fault. If an electric fan is fitted then that, too, might be the culprit if it's turning on too early – or more likely, not turning off at all! Finally, on an old engine – and all TR6s are now 'old' – the alloy thermostat housing itself might be suffering from internal corrosion, causing the thermostat to jam. Replace it if need be.

4 The water pump

There are three main parts to the water pump assembly: the cast-iron housing, which feeds water into the engine block and has the outlet connection to the bottom radiator hose; the water pump itself, with the four-bladed impeller; and the steel

6.3: The water pump and its housing.

drive pulley. By and large, TR6 water pumps are reliable, but if the drivebelt is over tightened, it can place unacceptable extra strain on the pumps bearing, causing it to fail. Earlier TR4-style water pumps could be greased, but TR6 units are sealed for life units. Another failure that can happen is with the woodruff key that holds the pulley in place on the shaft; this can wear its locating groove, causing it to slip, and eventually fail completely. If the pump needs to be replaced, it's a case of slackening and removing the fan belt from the pulley, undoing the three locating bolts – taking care over the lower one as it can be a bit of a pig to get a spanner on – and removing it from the engine.

At this stage, you might want to replace the iron water pump housing with a new alloy one. It's also advisable to fit a new water pump with an uprated impeller (with six blades rather than the usual four), and finish it all off with an alloy pulley.

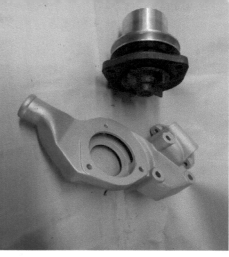

6.4: This alloy pump housing and pulley saves weight. The pump itself is an original four-bladed impeller.

5 Coolant

Until the advent of waterless cooling products, tap water mixed with antifreeze was the obvious choice for all motorists. The author has tried waterless cooling in both road and racing cars, but has since reverted to using the water and antifreeze solution. Since water boils at 100 degrees (which is plenty hot enough), any problem with the car's cooling system will soon become apparent, whereas with the waterless system, any problems with

6.5: The standard heater valve can be very hard to shut off completely.

6.6: This aftermarket heater valve has replaced the standard fitment and has a much better operation.

the engine will be much harder and take much longer to detect. This is not to say that waterless cooling is to be avoided, but it's an expensive replacement for an already well-proven system for cooling an engine.

6 The heater

An often overlooked part of the car's cooling system is the heater, yet it contains the same water that circulates around the engine; It, too, needs to be kept in good shape. The standard two-speed Smiths heater was quite adequate when the cars were new, but anyone who expects it to be on par with modern air-conditioning will be in for a big disappointment! Poor heating performance can be attributed to:

1. A faulty thermostat preventing the right coolant temperature being reached.

2. The electric blower motor might also be inoperative, probably due to the switch being broken.
3. The control flaps might be stuck or not opening fully.
4. The heater valve may not be fully turned on, or stuck in the closed position.
5. A blocked heater matrix.

The latter is basically a very small radiator which acts as the heat exchanger, and can suffer from the same faults as the full-sized radiator. The first sign of leaks in the heater matrix is often wet carpet!

The rubber pipes passing through the bulkhead are also often overlooked. The two located under the bulkhead are out of sight, but with age, they can harden and crack. The same applies to those in the engine bay, but a close visual inspection here will give an indication of what the internal pipes might be like.

If undertaking a full rebuild, it's often advisable to fit an uprated heater from one of the aftermarket suppliers. The author runs a three-speed Clayton heater, which means that the original two-speed toggle switch had to be replaced with a rotary one. That in itself is no great hardship, but it does affect the look for those interested in keeping things original.

The heater valve on a TR is a pretty poor affair, being cable operated from a push/pull knob on the plinth on the centre console. It's mostly easy to open, but closing it fully is another matter. An aftermarket slide type valve makes for a much better replacement for every day operation.

Finally, don't forget that there are two drain taps fitted to a TR6: one at the bottom of the radiator, and one on the right-hand rear of the engine block, tucked away under the inlet manifolds.

The TR6 has coil springs at the front (and rear), and is fitted with direct action rack and pinion steering, mounted immediately ahead of the engine, but behind the radiator. The stub axle is mounted on the vertical kingpin, and this carries the wheel hub and bearing assembly. Standard shock absorbers are non-adjustable, and are mounted inside the coil springs on a pressed steel spring pan bolted to the lower wishbones. A front anti-roll bar is fitted as standard, mounted to the chassis via the radiator

sumpguard, with the ends of the bar being connected by drop links to the lower wishbones. The trunnions are sometimes fitted with a grease nipple, but not all cars have these, a sure sign they have been replaced at some point in time; the same can be said of the trackrod ends.

7.1: The front suspension setup showing upper and lower wishbones, coil spring and the yellow shock absorber.

1 Common problems

The front suspension on any car has to do a lot of very hard work, so it's important to keep it in good working order. The front suspension on a TR6 is of the double wishbone type and can easily be maintained by any competent home mechanic. The Achilles heel of this setup is wear on the trunnion and kingpin assembly due to a lack of lubrication – this will be addressed in greater detail below. Other problems manifest as 'woolly' steering caused by excessive play in the steering geometry. Any 'clunks' from the front suspension need to be investigated immediately as that can be sign of wear in bushes. Finally, corrosion where the lower wishbone connects to the chassis is not unknown, and in some cases the whole of the front suspension has sheared off, with dramatic results for both car and driver!

2 The coil springs

You might think that there isn't very much that can go wrong with a coil spring, and by and large this is true. They have been known to crack, though, usually after hitting a large pothole at speed. When that happens, the affected corner will sag, and steering will become hard, if not impossible. When rebuilding a car, it is important not to confuse the front springs with the rear ones, as they are of different lengths. Springs sometimes have different colour paint on them – red, yellow and blue being known to the author – which indicates different spring rates. The springs should be fitted with rubber rings to prevent noise and chaffing with the lower spring pan and the top mounting. Alloy blocks of different thicknesses can also be placed into the top of the spring to get the correct ride height. Never replace just one affected spring. Always replace them in pairs – either both front or both rear at the same time. The same can be said for the shock absorbers.

3 The shock absorbers

Oil-filled telescopic shock absorbers are fitted to the front suspension and they sit inside the coil springs. Held at the bottom by four bolts to the lower spring pan, and a single locking nut at the top of the spring tower, they are very easy to replace with adjustable ones like Koni or Spax.

A general service should check that the securing nuts are still tight, and that there are no signs of oil weeping from the units. A quick test to see if they are working properly is to 'bounce' the front wing – if it continues to bounce more than one and a half times, check the shockers and replace if necessary. Always replace shock absorbers and

springs in matched pairs. Failure to do so will result in poor handling and extra wear on the system.

4 Kingpin (vertical link) & stub axle assembly

This is one of the most critical parts of the front suspension, and probably where you will find most of the wear in the system. The kingpin, or vertical link as it is sometimes called, is a single forging with three distinct areas to it. There is the hole in the top – which takes the upper universal joint for the top wishbones – then there is the stub axle itself, and finally, the lower threaded part that screws into the trunnion. It is this lower threaded bit which can suffer from most of the wear associated with kingpins; wear here can occur very rapidly, and the damaged thread can sometimes appear 'waisted' along its length. The author's own

7.3: The lower wishbone mountings are prone to failure, but reinforcing brackets can be fitted.

7.2: The vertical link and trunnion. The threaded part can wear badly if not kept lubricated.

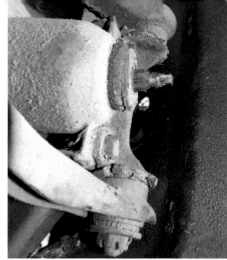

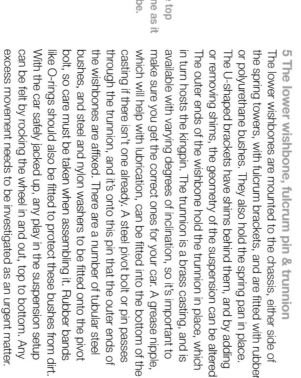

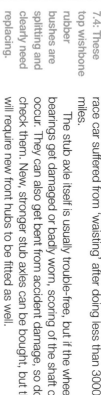

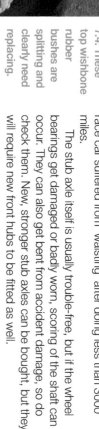

7.4: These top wishbone rubber bushes are splitting and clearly need replacing.

7.5: The top wishbone as it should be.

race car suffered from 'waisting' after doing less than 3000 miles.

The stub axle itself is usually trouble-free, but if the wheel bearings get damaged or badly worn, scoring of the shaft can occur. They can also get bent from accident damage, so do check them. New, stronger stub axles can be bought, but they will require new front hubs to be fitted as well.

5 The lower wishbone, fulcrum pin & trunnion

The lower wishbones are mounted to the chassis, either side of the spring towers, with fulcrum brackets, and are fitted with rubber or polyurethane bushes. They also hold the spring pan in place. The U-shaped brackets have shims behind them, and by adding or removing shims, the geometry of the suspension can be altered. The outer ends of the wishbone hold the trunnion in place, which in turn hosts the kingpin. The trunnion is a brass casting, and is available with varying degrees of inclination, so it's important to make sure you get the correct ones for your car. A grease nipple, which will help with lubrication, can be fitted into the bottom of the casting if there isn't one already. A steel pivot bolt or pin passes through the trunnion, and it's onto this pin that the outer ends of the wishbones are affixed. There are a number of tubular steel bushes, and steel and nylon washers to be fitted onto the pivot bolt, so care must be taken when assembling it. Rubber bands like O-rings should also be fitted to protect these bushes from dirt. With the car safely jacked up, any play in the suspension setup can be felt by rocking the wheel in and out, top to bottom. Any excess movement needs to be investigated as an urgent matter.

6 The upper wishbone

The upper wishbone is formed by a two-part steel pressing, which are handed, so make sure you assemble them the correct

way round. They fit onto the chassis by the upper fulcrum pin, a separate forging held in place by four bolts on top of the spring tower. Two-part 'top hat' style rubber bushes are used here, which, as the photo shows, are prone to wear. Meanwhile, the outer end of the upper wishbone takes the universal ball joint which fits into the kingpin. The ball joint is fixed to the wishbone by two long bolts that pass through the ball joint. A grease nipple can be fitted to this top ball joint to aid lubrication.

7 Front anti-roll bar

An anti-roll bar was added as standard to the TR5, and this was carried over to the TR6. Its purpose is to help control the front wheels when cornering, by transferring the cornering forces from the inside wheel to the outer wheel. It's fitted to the radiator sumpguard by clamps, and to the leading lower wishbones by short articulated vertical links. Apart from checking the condition of the mounting rubbers and the vertical links, no other maintenance is required, although over time it might have become distorted. This can be checked by removing the bar from the car and laying it on a flat surface. Both ends of the bar should be on the ground. If they aren't, it has become twisted and should be replaced.

8 The wheel bearings

There are two bearings in each wheel hub – an inner and an outer ball race. As long as the bearings are correctly set up, and not over tightened or too slack, they should perform without any trouble. Original equipment (OE) bearings were very good, and Timken make very good bearings, too, but there are a number of

7.7: A RHD steering rack and its mountings. Note the position of the oil cooler bolted to the radiator sump guard.

7.8: Note the rubber coupling between the upper and lower steering columns and the adjustable clamp to the left of it.

7.9: The lower steering column joint.

inferior bearings now on the market; the temptation to fit these is another example of false economy.

With the car safely jacked-up, if the bearings are showing signs of wear, a spin of the wheel will cause rumbles from the bearings. A further test is to hold the wheel with your hands in the 9 o'clock/3 o'clock position, and rock it. If you feel any play, this will show that the wheel bearing needs tightening up. Regular greasing is also a must if the bearings are to be maintained properly.

9 The steering assembly

The rack and pinion assembly is a very reliable unit, and the only real wear and tear is found at the trackrod ends, which occasionally need replacing, or if one of the rubber gaiters splits, allowing dirt and grime to enter the rack. The trackrod ends can, or should, be fitted with grease nipples, and be regularly checked for wear. This can best be done with an assistant to waggle the steering wheel while you feel for any movement in the ball joint. Trackrod end wear can make itself evident by sloppy steering, uneven tyre wear and clunking noises. The rack itself is clamped down to the front crossmember with special U-bolt clamps. These pose no problem, but the rubber inserts can deteriorate, and will need checking.

10 The steering column

Triumph was well ahead of the game when it came to collapsible steering columns. The TR6 steering assembly is actually made up of an upper and lower column. The upper column is shown in Figure 7.8, protruding through the bulkhead. The lower column is a steel rod, with a universal coupling fitted at the lower end and a rubber donut where it joins the upper column.

It's important to see that the pinch bolt on the lower coupling is taken all the way through, and secured with a self-locking nut (see 7.9). It's also important to check that the upper donut has an earth strap fitted, so that the earth circuit is complete. The upper column has a sliding joint secured by a clamp, that allows for the column to be adjusted for length and reach. If the steering wheel shows signs of excess up-and-down movement, then the top bush fitted inside the upper column is worn, and should be replaced.

11 Steering alignment

Maintaining the correct castor and camber angles is important, but modern laser tracking devices very often do not measure these. As the TR6 has a proper chassis, it is possible that any previous accident damage has twisted the chassis out of true. Only a proper drop check can verify this, but if the steering on the car continues to feel vague after replacing any worn out parts, this should be considered and undertaken by a specialist.

12 Improvements that can be made

For ordinary road car use, the standard front suspension and steering setup is fine. If you are finding it hard to park, one option is to fit a powered steering rack. These can be electric or hydraulic in function, but neither is going to be a cheap conversion. However, if the car is to be prepared for competition, there are a number of options to 'sharpen' things up. Fitting a smaller steering wheel and a 'quick rack' (usually taken from a Triumph Spitfire) will increase steering response. Alloy hub carriers will reduce unsprung weight, and larger stub axles and wheel bearings can also be fitted. The top wishbones can also be reshaped to increase negative camber. Alternatively, rose-jointed top wishbones can be employed, while lower wishbones can be shimmed accordingly. Higher rate competition springs are a popular modification, too, but ride comfort would be sacrificed. A stiffer and larger diameter anti-roll bar can also be fitted, as shown in 7.5, to improve handling through the corners.

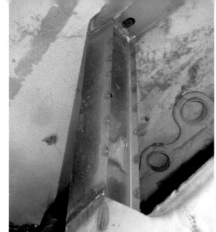

8.1: TR6 independent rear suspension. Note the non-standard telescopic shock absorbers.

8.2: This chassis member, which secures the trailing arm, had to be replaced due to rust.

With its independent semi trailing arm and coil spring rear suspension setup, the TR6 possessed a much more comfortable ride than some of its contemporaries – like the MGB, which still had solid beam axles. When IRS was first introduced into the TR range on the TR4A, motoring critics hailed it as a great step forward in sports car design, but by the end of the TR6's seven-year production run that praise had become less so, as chassis design had improved considerably over the years. The separate chassis of the TR was by now already an obsolete method of sports car construction, and modern suspension systems were able to give a much smoother ride. That said, the TR6 is still a very comfortable car to drive, and that is, in no small part, due to the design of the rear suspension. The trailing arms are large, heavy-duty alloy castings. Each trailing arm has two hard rubber bushes pressed into them. These bushes take the U-bracket mountings, which are then bolted to the car's chassis rails, and secure the rear suspension (see photo 8.3). The arm also acts as the hub carrier for the drive shafts, and the spring and shock absorber pick-up points. The coil spring fits neatly into the recess cast in the arm, while the shock absorber, which is fixed to the chassis, uses a vertical link to connect it to the trailing arm.

Suspension problems

Any creaks, rattles or groans coming from the rear end will be a sign that something is not quite right, so early investigation is advised. The alloy trailing arms in particular can be vulnerable to damage and cracking if they hit something hard enough.

One of the main things to look out for is corrosion where

8.4: The Armstrong lever shock absorber mountings.

8.3: The U-brackets holding the trailing arms to the chassis can be clearly seen in this shot, and can be altered to change camber angles.

should be okay inside. However, if the corrosion is bad to the extent that holes are beginning to appear in the chassis rails, then some serious welding will be required.

Stripping the rear suspension down is quite straightforward, but care should be taken. A jack should be used to take up the strain on the spring before attempting to remove the vertical links. Removal of the rear hubs is quite straightforward, too, but care must be taken when refitting them, as too much effort in replacing the studs can strip the threads in the alloy hub. For this reason, always use a torque wrench and consult the workshop manual for the correct setting.

Replacing the rubber bushes can be done at home with the aid of a heavy-duty vice and some steel tubing, but it's not that easy. A proper workshop press will have them out and new ones fitted in a fraction of the time, so it's worth going to see your local garage to get it done. Original spec factory items are available, but most people these days fit polyurethane bushes instead.

the trailing arms bolt into the chassis. This is a very vulnerable point as cornering loads can be quite high. The bolts holding the U-brackets – to which the trailing arms are fixed – pass all the way through the chassis, and are easily removable if doing a rebuild. Inside the box section of the chassis, there are some pressings which the bolts also pass through, and these can rust quite badly. They are there to prevent the chassis becoming distorted when the bolts are done up tight, and provide a sort of tube for the bolt to pass through. As it is impossible to check on their condition without cutting the chassis open, if these sections of the chassis are in good condition, you can assume that all

They give a slightly harder ride but have a better life. It's your choice.

Rear springs are often replaced with stronger, higher-rated, 'competition' ones, but this can be a mistake as the ride quality will suffer. You need to ask yourself, what end use will the car have? If it's just for touring then there is nothing wrong with the standard setup.

The vertical links have a rubber joint which can, and does, perish to the extent that the links can come apart and just drop out. Rose-jointed versions are available, but again, unless competition is your aim, replacing them with standard ones will suffice.

The lever arm shock absorbers are a throwback to the earliest TR2. They can work loose, so one tip is to replace the standard bolts with longer ones – which then pass through the chassis

8.5: A vertical shocker conversion.

mounting – and fit a Nyloc nut on them (see photo 8.3). They can also leak, and it's worth checking and topping up the fluid in them from time to time. This can be done by undoing the small nut on the top of the shock absorber.

However, it is possible to convert your lever arm shockers to telescopic types, and a number of retro-fitting kits are available. One type fits the shocker inside the coil spring, while another fits it to the rear of the trailing arm. The latter type will require a mounting on the wheelarch, while the former can use the spring mounting on the chassis bridge.

Finally, although never offered as a factory option, the fitment of a rear anti-roll bar is favoured by some enthusiasts. These, too, utilise the same vertical link pick-up point, and are fixed to the chassis with brackets which can be either welded or bolted on.

8.6: The rear anti-roll bar is bolted to the chassis and trailing arms.

9 The propshaft, differential & rear hubs

9.1: Note that the bolts are passed through from the propshaft side.

The drive line

Unlike the live axle TR4s that preceded the TR6, the independent rear suspension setup of the TR4A, 5, and 6 was able to replace the solid cast axle with a much more compact differential housing and a swing axle with sliding joint half shafts. Although more complex than the old live axle setup, the IRS systems gave a much better ride, as the revised chassis design allowed for much greater wheel travel.

1 Common problems: oil leaks, final drive noise & halfshaft clunk

Oil leaks in the drive line can only come from one source: the differential. The differential gears can also be a source of noise and the halfshafts can wear badly. All of these areas will be addressed, but let us look at the first part of the final drive system: the propeller shaft.

2 The propeller shaft

The propeller shaft is a two-piece sliding joint affair that benefits from being regularly lubricated with grease. Fitted at both ends with universal joint (UJ) couplings, it is advisable to try to fit joints which can be greased if possible. Wear in the UJ can cause the propshaft to rumble and vibrate. When UJs are worn, a 'clunk' can often be heard when pulling away from rest, or when changing gear, but in the worst case, the UJs can break up and cause the propshaft to flail in the tunnel, with a somewhat alarming noise!

While it is easier to remove the propshaft and replace the UJs

when taking the gearbox out, it can be done from underneath the car, as it's only four bolts at each end of the shaft. Care should be taken to replace the Nyloc nuts and bolts the correct way round.

3 The differential

The TR6 differential is housed in a cast iron and alloy casing, bolted to the chassis by the four prominent lugs on the casing. It's easy to remove from underneath the car, but it is advisable to undo the four bolts securing the propeller shaft, and the eight bolts securing the halfshafts to the differential first, before attempting to remove the differential itself.

The differential itself was available with 3.7 or 4.1 ratios, and it is susceptible to crown wheel and pinion wear. If a tooth has broken on the crown wheel or pinion then the rumbling noise will

9.3: Left: A crown wheel and pinion set. Note the roller bearing cage. Right the differential cage.

be very apparent to the driver! Replacing and setting up a new crown wheel and pinion is a specialist job, as the gears have to mesh perfectly. The three differential oil seals are also prone to leak, so it's important to check that the diff is topped up with the correct oil. There are various gear oils on the market, but this is one application when EP or extreme pressure oil can be used safely. Also, when fitting new bearings and oil seals to the differential, please ensure they are fitted the correct way round.

4 The halfshafts

With the IRS system replacing the solid beam axle of the earlier TRs, it was necessary to fit two-piece sliding splined halfshafts to all the IRS TRs, with UJs at both ends. The sliding shaft joint is protected by a rubber bellow to prevent dirt and grit entering the splines. It's important to keep the spline well greased in order to prevent spline lock up under hard cornering. An indicator of worn splines is a distinct 'clunk' on acceleration.

While standard spec halfshafts are readily available, uprated halfshafts with Teflon-coated splines can also be fitted as a direct replacement, as can those which replace the UJs with constant velocity joints. These modifications are designed to help prevent spline lock-up if the shafts are worn or badly greased.

Earlier TR types were fitted with a grease nipple on the propshaft, and the UJs often had the same provision for greasing.

9.4: A half shaft extended to show the sliding splines.

9.6 shows a UJ that has had the grease nipple replaced with a set screw. While it has had the grease nipple replaced with a set screw. While it might be a bit of trouble to fit grease nipples to all of your UJs, it's well worth it, and they will be much better than the so-called sealed-for-life units.

5 Rear hub carriers & hubs

The large cast alloy trailing arms, also act as the hub carrier, spring pan, and shock absorber mounting. The hub carriers themselves are attached to the chassis by two U-brackets, which can be set up to induce both camber and toe-in angles. While these mounting brackets are themselves very solid items, it is where they bolt through the chassis that they can suffer badly from internal corrosion. It's not unknown for a swing axle to be pulled clear of the chassis (with disastrous results) due to chassis failure at this point.

The rear hubs on a TR6 carry the brakes and are bolted to the

alloy hub carriers by eight studs, which have a tendency to strip their threads if over tightened. Replacing the inner and outer hub bearings is also a job for an engineering shop equipped with a heavy duty hydraulic press.

45

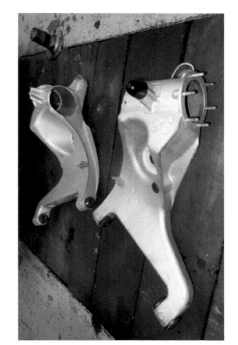

9.6: A set screw has replaced the grease nipple on this half shaft's universal joint.

9.5: The constant velocity half shafts shown here have replaced the original standard sliding shafts but its an expensive option.

9.7: These cast alloy hub carriers have had their rubber bushes replaced with modern polybushes. Note also the black rebound rubber on top of the hub and the six studs which secure the hub itself.

9.8: A rear hub. Replacing the inner and outer bearings is not really a DIY job.

9.9: Spilned hubs need regular greasing. The author uses Copperslip but any heavy duty grease will suffice. This one utilises the spacer mentioned above.

6 Wire wheels

Both the front and rear hubs can be adapted to carry wire wheels, and the standard method of carrying out this modification is to place the splined hub adaptor on the hub and use the special chamfered nuts that come with the conversion kit. The excess thread then has to be cut off, otherwise the wire wheel

won't fit. Alternatively, thin ¼-inch spacers can be fitted to the hub prior to bolting the hub adaptor in place. By doing so, it does place an extra load on the hub bearing, and the track becomes slightly wider, but the impact is negligible. The advantage of using these spacers is that you can revert back to steel or alloy wheels without having to replace all the wheel studs.

Wire wheel hubs are also splined and can wear badly if not kept well greased. It is important to torque the hub nuts correctly, as if they work loose, the wheel may become detached from the car, with disastrous consequences.

Also, when fitting splines for the first time to a car that has previously only had steel or alloy wheels, do make sure you have them on the correct side, as the wheel retaining threads are handed. I know from experience how a hurried conversion can potentially cost you your car when a wheel becomes loose! The chrome nuts are clearly marked which way they should be done up. The one shown here in 9.9 is from the near side of a RHD car.

9.10: This three-eared wheel spinner on a centre-laced 6 JK wheel rim has replaced the octagonal nut usually found on a TR6.

10 The braking system

The system overview

The TR6 is equipped with power/servo-assisted disc brakes at the front, and twin shoe brake drums on the rear. It's a dual circuit system so if one circuit fails then you still have a 'reserve' in place to halt your progress. The pipe work for the system starts at the master cylinder and is fed down towards the chassis rails. From there, it goes along the chassis rails and is retained by steel clips to the respective brake discs and drums, where flexible hoses make the final connections to the callipers and pistons.

1 Brake fluid

When TR6s were rolling off the production line, the braking system was filled with a mineral-based brake fluid, but it's hydroscopic nature means that the system could be contaminated with water by absorption. Water in the braking system can cause premature wear in the rear wheel cylinders and front brake callipers. It also means that the boiling point of the brake fluid gets gradually lower, until it reaches the point when vapour in the system creates a 'soft' pedal and may not work at all. In really cold weather, the water could also freeze and cause ice crystals to form in the brake lines.

Today, many owners have drained their systems and replaced the mineral-based fluid with a silicone-based one which does not attract moisture. This in turn prevents any internal corrosion of the steel brake pipes, but it's important that the two types of fluid do not mix, as they are not compatible with each other. If you are contemplating upgrading your system to use silicone fluid in your car, then make sure to flush the mineral oil from the system

completely. This is easier said than done, but an air line can help. Also, mineral oil ought to be changed at regular service intervals, which are usually every three years or 30,000 miles, but with classic cars rarely making such mileage these days, it's better to check your system out at the start of every year. Finally, mineral fluid should never come into contact with the paintwork of your car. If it does, clean it off immediately with warm water as it can be a very effective paint remover! Silicone fluids, you will be glad to hear, don't have such a nasty side effect.

2 Fluid leakages

It is advisable to check the level in the reservoir regularly, and any noticeable loss of fluid should be investigated immediately. Leaks can manifest under the servo and at joint connections in the pipe work. Leaks can also be traced to the front callipers and rear wheel cylinders. It should go without saying that it's not advisable to drive the car if you do find a leak. However, if a leak manifests while on the road, it may result in steering pulling to one side or a spongy feel to the brake pedal. Do not, however, confuse a longer pedal travel with leaking brakes. As brake linings wear, the pedal will move a bit further. If in doubt, check the system over thoroughly.

3 The master cylinder & servo

The large, plastic brake fluid reservoir sitting on top of the master cylinder is one of the first things you see upon opening the bonnet of a TR6, so it's very hard to miss. The cylinder itself is attached directly to the brake servo, which in turn is fixed to the bulkhead by four bolts which pass through an alloy spacer. The two pipes coming out of the cylinder form the dual circuit system, which goes to the front and rear brakes.

A look inside the reservoir shows a dividing 'wall' between the two systems, and it's important to check that the brake fluid is at the correct level on both sides of the 'wall.' Fluid levels can and will drop as brake pads wear, so regular inspection of the fluid level is required. Any sudden drop in levels, or a spongy pedal must be investigated immediately as a fractured brake pipe may be the cause. By and large though, brake master cylinders are reliable units, but seals can fail, and fluid can leak back into the servo unit itself. A telltale sign of a leak can be fluid running down the brake pedal inside the car. Removal and replacement of the brake master cylinder and servo is straightforward if you follow the workshop manual. The servo itself is operated by vacuum from the engine via a rubber hose.

10.1: Clutch master cylinder on the left. Brake master cylinder on the right.

10.2: The disc brake rotor and calliper. Note the stainless brake hose and Kunifer brake pipe.

4 Front disc brakes

Historically, TRs were one of the first production cars to be fitted with disc brakes, first appearing on the TR3 in 1956. Those fitted to the TR6 are very different to the early cars, having a slightly reduced disc diameter (10^{13}/$_{16}$-inch as opposed to 11-inch), and a much smaller and lighter brake calliper. The discs themselves are attached to the front hubs and have a dust plate fitted to the inside of the disc.

The callipers house two pistons, one on either side of the disc, and for its day, the car had pretty good stopping power. The brake pads are held in place by long pins, which are retained by P-clips, with anti-rattle/squeal shims also fitted. These shims can benefit from a smear of copper ease, but be careful not to get any on the friction material itself.

Approximately 70 per cent of the braking effort is undertaken by the front brakes, and there are several ways in which the front brakes can be upgraded. The easiest upgrade is to cross drill the discs themselves, as this will aid the removal of water, gas and brake dust, but it will not radically improve braking performance. To do that you either need to fit thicker ventilated discs, with a suitably wider calliper or, better still, fit larger discs, again with an appropriate brake calliper. Callipers, too, can benefit from an upgrade from two-pot to four-pot pistons, but these will cost you time and some serious money.

Brake pads and rear linings should be replaced at the same time on both sides of the car to prevent asymmetrical braking. Fitting a different type of brake material can be done, and there are various options on the market, but ALWAYS check that whatever brake pads or lining you use are genuine parts, as there are a lot of fakes out there. Bad spelling can be an indicator of a fake part.

5 Rear drum brakes

With the car jacked up and the rear wheels removed, the rear brake drums are exposed. These are cast iron units held in place by two countersunk machine screws. With the handbrake off – and remembering to chock the front wheels – the drums can be eased off to expose the back plate, brake shoes, adjusters, and the dual action piston. In normal service, all that is required is a clean up of any accumulated brake dust and dirt. Replacing the brake shoes is a simple affair if you follow the workshop manual. A dab of grease on the shoe pivot points will help, but again, take care not to get any on the brake linings themselves.

There isn't much you can do to improve the brakes themselves, but the drums can be replaced with Alfin-type alloy drums, which are available from a number of TR specialists (see Chapter 16).

10.3: Rear brake drum.

10.4: The rear brake shoes and adjuster.

6 The handbrake

An important part of the MOT test, the handbrake is often overlooked. Located on the transmission tunnel, its simple workings are concealed by its 'glove.' The brake is operated by a push button spring-loaded ratchet, and a coupler holds the ends of the two handbrake cables, which pass through the lower rear bulkhead. The other ends of the cable hold the brackets that fit onto the actuating levers of the brake shoes with a clevis pin. Cables can stretch and lose tension. They can also be damaged by debris thrown up from the road, so it's important to check their condition and operation. Replacement is one of the easiest DIY jobs you can undertake on a TR.

7 Brake light operation

Hidden under the dashboard and in the footwell of the TR6 is the switch which operates the brake lights when pressure is applied to the pedal. Out of sight is often out of mind, but it's worth checking that the switch is in good working order if your brake lights are playing up. To check the switch, turn the ignition circuit on and connect both terminals. If the lights come on, the switch is faulty and needs to be replaced. The lights should only illuminate when the brake pedal is pressed.

8 Brake problems

Brake problems can manifest themselves in a number of ways. Leaks, noises, vibration, and poor control are all symptoms of a problem that can be traced back to your brakes.

Loss of brake fluid from the main reservoir has already been covered, but leaks can occur at any pipe union, at the rear wheel cylinders, the callipers, and at the flexible hoses. Excessive brake pedal travel is another sign of a potential leak within the system. Any sign of such a leak needs to be attended to immediately.

Noisy brakes can be an indication that the brake lining material is seriously worn. What you can hear is the metal part of the brake pad scouring the disc, or the rivets of the brake shoe making contact with the iron drum. Immediate replacement of the affected parts is the answer.

Vibration under braking can also be caused by badly worn brake drums and discs. Disc brakes which are showing signs of wear will seriously affect your braking performance, and scored discs are a sign of uneven pad wear. The brake pedal will feel

10.5: Front brakes can be up-rated by fitting ventilated disc rotors.

uncomfortable under pressure. Remember, too, that brake discs can and will rust if left unused for long periods. A car that has been left standing over the winter can even find the brake pads seized onto the disc. A scored disc can be skimmed, but TR discs are not all that thick to begin with, and with new discs readily available, it is in my mind false economy to skim them.

It is also advisable to check the run out on the disc as it is possible for a disc to 'warp' if subjected to very heavy braking and sudden cooling. This can be done with a dial gauge and they should be not be more than eight thou out of true. Similarly, the rear brake drums can wear to an oval shape, and while these too can be machined back to true, fitting a new Alfin type drum would be an easier fix.

If the car pulls to one side under braking it could be due to uneven wear on the front pads, a sticking piston in the brake calliper, or even a leak on the opposite side. If the brakes check out okay then other causes need to be investigated. Try checking your tyre pressures, and look for mismatched front tyres and worn steering or suspension components.

If the brakes are found to be sticking, the cause may be a

sticking or seized wheel cylinder at the rear, or a deteriorating flexible hose. While it might look okay on the outside, the inside of the hose might be breaking up and acting as a sort of non-return valve. Stainless steel braided hoses are a popular replacement for rubber hoses, and are available in sets for your car.

Overall, regular servicing and inspection of all the braking system components will ensure that you have trouble-free motoring. A bit of grease goes a long way in keeping the system in good condition, and cars that are laid up for the winter need to be paid greater attention when being put back on the road again in the spring.

Finally, don't forget to check your pipework for corrosion. Older cars often had their brake pipes covered in underseal, which can also be used to conceal badly corroded pipes. If rebuilding the car, it's a good idea to replace all the steel pipe work with Kunifer pipe; this is a copper alloy and is much stronger than some of the pure copper brake pipe kits that are available. Fitting stainless steel braided brake hoses, as mentioned above, is also a good idea.

All TR6s are fitted with 15-inch diameter road wheels, but there are a number of variations. Very early cars were fitted with the 'Rostyle' polished stainless steel trims, as fitted to the TR5 on a 5-inch rim, and these are now quite sought after. The TR6 finally got its own 5.5-inch steel road wheels towards the end of 1969. These were fitted with a black plastic centre knave plate, with heavy chrome wheel nuts, but by 1973 the black knave plates were replaced with silver ones. Also available on later cars fitted with steel wheels was a 'bling ring' chrome insert.

As the steel wheels are only painted, rust can be a problem if left unchecked, but shot blasting and powder coating can rectify that.

What is harder to fix is a buckled wheel rim caused by kerbing. A buckled rim can cause steering vibration, and wheels should be checked on both sides for damage.

1 Wire wheels

72-spoke wire wheels were always a factory option, and were available in painted or chrome finish. The two-eared locking nut – which was always a feature on TRs – was replaced with an octagonal nut, and needed a specially shaped tool to remove them. Wire wheels also required special splined hub adaptors (see Chapter 9, photo 9.8). While wire wheels can transform the look of the car, they require much more maintenance than steel wheels.

Cleaning a wire wheel properly is a very time-consuming task; even with the aid of a power washer, it can be hard to remove all traces of brake dust, which collects by the spokes. Wire wheels

11.1: A 15in Rostyle wheel trim as found on the earliest TR6s. Not to be confused with those used on 2.5 saloons, GT6 or the Vitesse.

11.2: This pre-1973 TR6 wheel can be identified by its black centre knave plate. Later cars had silver ones. A chrome 'bling ring' could also be added to enhance the appearance of the wheel (see photo 11.4).

are also more prone to accident damage from kerbing. A twisted wire wheel will make the steering seem very heavy.

The spokes can become loose and the locating splines can also wear badly if not properly lubricated. Loose spokes can be identified by a tinkling sound as the load is taken up under acceleration. Chrome wires are also more susceptible to broken spokes as the chroming process makes the steel more brittle. Clunks in the drive line under acceleration and braking can be an indication of worn splines.

Wire wheels also required the use of an inner tube and a rubber spoke protector, but modern wires can now run tubeless tyres, as they are fitted with a nylon band that covers the spoke fittings in the well of the wheel.

Balancing a wire wheel correctly is very important, and not every tyre fitter has the correct cone adaptor to spin them up to speed. Modern balancing machines, though, can now accurately measure run-out, and balance both the inside and outside of the wheel.

2 Aftermarket wheels

It is well known that wheels can transform the look of your car, and TRs are no exception to this. One option to enhance the look of the TR6 wheels was to add what is sometime referred to as a 'bling ring,' actually a chrome insert fitted to the rim of the wheel.

Alloy wheels were actually fitted to US spec TR4s as American Racing wheels, and they are now quite sought-after in Britain, too.

11.3: 72-spoke wire wheels with the octagonal nut.

11.4: A 'bling ring' fitted to a TR6. They are very much a 'Marmite' option in that you either love them or hate them.

Another popular style of wheel that many TR owners fit to their cars is Minilite replica wheels. These alloy wheels have eight large spokes and are much easier to keep clean. However, being alloy they are more susceptible to kerbing and alloy corrosion, which can cause problems in sealing the tyre to the bead.

Whichever type of wheel you choose, it is important not to go overboard with them, and to pay attention to wheel offsets. A six-inch rim width can easily be accommodated by a TR6 but going too large with rim widths can place severe strain upon suspension components, which can then lead to front suspension failure.

11.5: Reproduction 'Minilite' style wheels are also available for splined hubs.

3 Tyres

A standard early factory-produced TR6 was fitted with 165 x 15in tyres but this was soon uprated to 185 x 15in tyres to go with the wider steel wheels of the TR6. Tyre technology increased greatly during the production life of the TR6. Tyre technology increased greatly during the production life of the TR6, and different tyres available that will fit the TR6, but Avon CR6ZZ are used by a number of road-going TRs in competition, as they combine grip and performance in the wet. However, the best advice is to always buy the best tyre you can afford, as it's the only thing that keeps you in contact with the road.

Going for a wide, low-profile tyre might look good but they place an enormous amount of strain on the suspension systems that weren't designed for it. The grip might be fantastic but they can also let go without warning too! Early TRs were designed during an age of cross ply tyres, which allowed for sliding around corners and were much more forgiving. Radial tyres, as fitted to the TR6, gave much higher levels of cornering, but modern compounds can exceed even those design limits. Understeer can quickly give way to oversteer with unexpected consequences.

If the car is going to be laid up for the winter, it's also a good idea to take the wheels off and lay the tyres flat to avoid flat-spotting the tyre (see Chapter 15). Finally, rather than fill the tyres with air, try to find a tyre dealer who will fill them with inert nitrogen. Air contains water vapour whereas nitrogen doesn't and pressures can be maintained more accurately.

12 Electrical system & instruments

All TRs use Lucas 12-volt electrical systems and there is a great deal of commonality of parts used between the cars. The TR6 uses a negative earth return from the battery, and power is supplied by an alternator driven from the fan belt. The main circuits are protected by fuses, which can be found in the fuse box fixed to the inner near side wing. The fuse box also has provision for two spare fuses to be carried internally. Electrical gremlins do rear their head from time to time, and because the condition of the wiring loom can deteriorate, it is usually one of the last things owners tend to replace.

Instrumentation came in two basic forms, which are easily identified from the colour of the instrument bezel, being black on early cars and chrome on later ones. US export cars also have some extra equipment – like hazard indicators – which were not fitted on UK spec cars, and these will be dealt with later.

1 Common problems: the battery

The TR6 battery is located on the bulkhead shelf under the bonnet. While this allows for very easy everyday access and much shorter leads to the starter motor, the battery can and does get hot, especially in summer when ambient temperatures are much higher. On a traditional lead acid battery, this can lead to the distilled water evaporating, so regular checks and top ups should be remembered. Distilled water used to be readily available from the garage forecourt, but as most garages now seem to be more interested in selling coffee rather than motoring aids, you can obtain your own supply simply by defrosting your freezer! Please do not use tap water!

Because modern batteries now tend to be sealed for life, you can't really maintain them, but a periodic check with a multimeter should see them show an output of more than 12 volts. One thing you can do, no matter what type of battery you have, is make sure the battery posts are kept clean: the same can be said for the clamps. The author recommends a good

12.1: The battery needs to be firmly clamped to the bulkhead.

smear of petroleum jelly, and, if possible, fitting some rubber terminal covers to the clamps in order to keep dirt away from them.

Another problem which is often overlooked is the condition of the earth strap. On the TR6, the earth is carried down to the body and then onto the back plate of the engine. The bolt securing it to the body must be clean, and do check that there isn't too much paint behind it. Experience has shown that after a rebuild and respray, a poor earth connection here can confound you if you have difficulty starting your car.

Finally, do make sure that the battery is kept secure at all times. The angle bracket provided does a good job on a standard size battery, but smaller, more modern units may be more difficult to secure. The fitment of a plastic battery box is always a good idea, as is clearly marking the battery terminals: red for positive, black or yellow for negative.

12.2 Heavy duty jump leads and trickle charger.

2 Jump leads & trickle charging

Cars that don't get a lot of use tend to have weak batteries and may require a jump start or the use of a portable starter pack to get going. Good quality jump leads are hard to find, but are easily identified by their relatively heavy weight. The thin wire leads that often come with some of the emergency packs sold at retail outlets are not really good enough.

When jump starting from another car, make sure the leads are fitted correctly. Fit the positive (+) red lead to the battery terminals first, then the negative (–) black lead making sure that the cable clamps don't touch any other part of either the car's engine or bodywork.

With the rescue car's engine running it should now be possible to start your own car. The rescue car should be revved up to about 1500rpm in order to offer a good output from its own generator. Once your car has started, disconnect the negative battery lead from your own car first, again making sure it doesn't touch the engine or bodywork, and remove the negative clamp from the other car. The positive lead can then be disconnected safely from both cars.

Charging a battery with a mains-powered battery charger should really be done with the battery taken out of the car. Batteries can give off fumes because of the electrolyte (sulphuric acid) used in them, and therefore charging in this way should be carried out in a well-ventilated place. Do NOT breathe in any fumes, and if you are unfortunate enough to spill any battery acid on you, wash it off immediately as it is highly corrosive.

Trickle charging is now a very popular method of keeping a car battery in good condition. There are various devices on the market, but those with a clear indicator of the charging level are among the most useful.

As above, make sure the connections are carried out correctly, and only turn the power on after the battery has been connected. Trickle chargers can be left on for long periods of time, but batteries work best when they can discharge and recycle, so once it's topped up why not take the car out for a run?

3 Battery acid spillage

If a plastic battery box or spill tray has been fitted, then any spillage from the battery should be safely contained. If the battery is just sitting on the bodywork, not only can the paintwork be damaged, but the acid can attack the steel work under it. Fumes from a battery can also affect the bulkhead, and this is usually most noticeable at the panel seam that runs behind the battery: it is advisable to leave the bonnet slightly open if being parked up in your garage.

4 Battery security

I have mentioned above the need to keep the battery secured, and the clamp provided will prevent it from moving about during normal day-to-day driving (see photo 12.1); in the event of an accident, and should the car turn over, that clamp might not be sufficient. The addition of some sturdy tie wraps looped over the top of the battery would improve things, and make sure that your terminal clamps are bolted on tight. A clamp that comes adrift in an accident could short out, and if there's a fuel leak from the high pressure system ... Well, it's best not to dwell on that scenario but fire and TRs do not mix!

5 The charging system

The alternator's job is to provide electricity to run the car's electrical systems and to keep the battery charged. The standard 15ACR/28amp and 16ACR/34amp alternators that were initially fitted to the TR6 (later cars had 17ACR/35amp ones) are perfectly capable of this, but I would recommend, as a minimum, to fit at least an 18ACR/45amp one.

With modern radios and multi-speaker systems plus the often needed addition of phone chargers and satellite navigation systems, the standard alternators fitted by Triumph really aren't up to the job anymore. With the electric fuel pump for the injection system needing at least 10amps to work properly, you can see that the TR's electrical system really begins to struggle.

Fortunately for us, the earlier TR6s are fitted with an ammeter, so you can see if the car is charging itself correctly. The needle should always be showing a positive charge, apart from on starting when it will, of course, be showing some discharging as the starter motor cranks the engine over.

The greatest load on the charging system is at night when it's more likely that everything will be operating. The headlights will be

12.3: The alternator.

on, if it's raining so will the wipers, the heater blower to demist the screen, as well as the aforementioned stereo and satnav systems; all will be requiring power and it is the alternator's job to provide it.

Alternators are pretty reliable units, but like all things mechanical, they can fail. Of course, the alternator is driven by the fan belt, and care must be taken not to run it too slack or, even worse, too tight! Over tensioning the fan belt can place strain on the alternator's bearings, which is usually accompanied by a loud screeching noise. If the alternator does pack up charging completely, it is usually a case of the diode pack failing; these can be replaced by any competent auto electrician.

If you decide to replace your alternator, there a number of options available. You can upgrade to a much higher-rated (amp wise) alternator that looks like an original, but may require a few

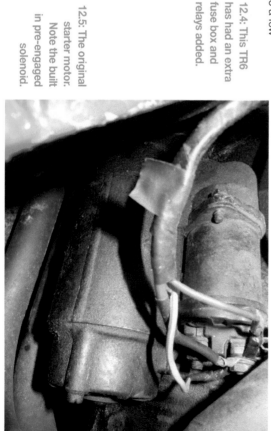

12.4: This TR6 has had an extra fuse box and relays added.

12.5: The original starter motor. Note the built in pre-engaged solenoid.

minor wiring modifications to the plug connector, or you can consider fitting a smaller, lightweight one available from the many TR specialists.

6 General electrical faults

The wiring system is probably the most neglected part on a classic car. All of the Lucas spade, screw or bullet connectors are potential weak links in the electrical system, and they can all suffer from corrosion. The connections that are exposed to road dirt and bad weather are especially susceptible, and should be checked first. The fuse holders themselves are protected, but the connectors are not, and over time many of the clear rubber Lucar spade connector covers split or go missing. A

quick start motor (see photo 12.6). These double reduction geared units spin the car's engine over much more quickly and draw less current. They are, to my mind, a must have, and all of my cars have been so equipped.

8 The instruments

Smiths' instruments were supplied as original equipment on the TR6. The dials are white numerals on black faces and all have flat glasses with either black or chrome bezels. The standard TR instrument layout is made up of matching 5-inch, cable-driven speedometer and tachometer (rev counter) placed directly in front of the driver, with four supplementary 2⅝-inch instruments for oil pressure, water temperature, fuel level, and an ammeter. On later cars, with the revised dials and chrome bezels, the ammeter was replaced with a volt meter.

Many cars have had their teak-finish dashboard replaced with burr walnut ones, and some owners have even replaced their gauges with cream-finished dials to give their car a more

12.7: The central instrument cluster from left to right: temperature, oil, fuel and amps, plus the rheostat for instrument lighting.

12.6: A reduction gear starter motor.

multimeter will help to identify any shortcomings in the circuits, but if the circuit is found to be sound, then it's probably the component itself which is at fault.

7 The starter motor

The original equipment starter motor is a pre-engaged unit with its own built-in solenoid. It's quite a heavy beast if you have to replace it, often requiring the removal of the exhaust downpipes to facilitate its removal. Starter motors can, of course, jam, and the old trick of giving it a belt with a hammer often releases it, but it's not advisable.

The motor draws a lot of current when starting, so it needs the battery to be in good condition if it's to spin the six-cylinder engine over.

If the engine has been modified with a higher compression ratio, it will place even more strain on the motor. My advice is to replace the motor with a much smaller, lighter, and more powerful modern look. However, the standard gauges work really well and need only careful cleaning to maintain their classic appearance. However, if the profile of the tyres has changed or a new gearbox/final drive ratio has been fitted then the speedometer will need to be re-calibrated if it is to give an accurate reading – handy when going past speed cameras! Similarly, the rev counter can be upgraded to an electric on, usually in conjunction with fitting a solid state distributor which negates the need for a drive cable.

If the drive cables are retained for the speedo and rev counter then it's worth paying attention to how they are routed in order to avoid kinking and/or chaffing as they pass through the bulkhead. The speedo cable is particularly susceptible to damage as it can hang down under the car's chassis.

12.8: An early TR6 dashboard showing the rocker switches for the washers/ wipers and a rare original steering wheel.

The angle drive (see photo 3.3) can also be a weak point on the speedo drive. As cables wear, the needles tend to fluctuate or bounce, so accurate reading can become difficult – *not very* handy when going past those speed cameras.

The odometer (trip meter) built into the speedometer is also prone to wear, and this is indicated by the numerals not lining up exactly. This is caused by the drive teeth becoming worn as drivers reset the trip back to zero. Meanwhile, the numerals on total mileage should remain in line, and if they don't then the mileage might well have been altered to give a lower reading.

The oil pressure gauge should read quite high on starting as oil pressure builds up: 80-100psi is quite normal. During normal running, oil pressure should never be less than 40psi at 2000rpm. Any lower than this, and it's likely that the main bearings are worn.

The fuel gauge is operated from a sender in the fuel tank and is generally a reliable unit. If it does need to be replaced, then the tank has to be removed in order to do so. This is a straightforward operation, but as usual, care must be taken to drain fuel from the tank, and it's *vitally important* to disconnect the battery first before attempting to remove it. After disconnecting the electrical connections to the sender unit and all the pipe unions that feed into the tank, it can be removed by undoing the six bolts securing it to the car's body. After replacing the sender unit, and with a new gasket seal, refitting the tank is a reversal of the above procedure.

The water temperature gauge has an electrical connection to its sender, which is mounted in the thermostat housing. The Lucar connection is easily dislodged so that no readings will show on the gauge. Other than that or a bulb failure, it's a reliable unit.

The ammeter/volt meter is the final instrument, and this can

12.11: The isolator cut-off switch.

give a good indication of the state of the electrical system. A reading of +15-20 amps should be seen on start-up as the charging system feeds back into the battery, and it should maintain a small positive reading of +2 amps or more when driving.

Other electrical switch gears that can cause problems are the wiper motor and the overdrive switches. The wiper motor is a two-speed unit operated by a rocker switch on early models, and a rotary switch on later ones. The early switches can be fragile, which is why they were replaced by the factory, but to upgrade an early car's switch to a later type switch would involve replacing the whole dashboard! Meanwhile, the overdrive that operates on 2nd, 3rd and 4th gears on the early cars, and 3rd and top only on later ones, can be plagued by poor connections to the isolator switches mounted on top of the gearbox. To fix these means removing a good portion of the car's interior,

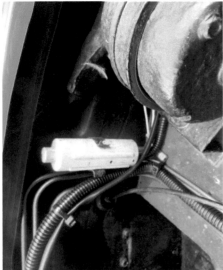

12.9: The two-speed wiper motor.

12.10: Two rocker switches for the wash/wipers show that this is a CP series car.

so it's a good idea to make sure the switches are shimmed correctly to operate in their respective gears, and, if possible, to wire them in place so that they cannot become loose. It's also a good idea to make sure the solenoids bullet connection is a secure one, too, and that there is enough slack in the overdrive cables feeding out of the gearbox cover and up to the steering column, as they have been known to come adrift at the bullet connectors.

US spec cars were also fitted with hazard indicators to comply with American regulations, and it was also possible to specify a basic air conditioning unit, which on an open top sports car in the 1970s must have been fairly novel.

Another electrical part which can create a problem is the ignition switch. On the early cars with a dash mounted switch, the barrels can wear, and original spec switches with FS series keys are no longer available. The replacement switches are rather

poor quality and don't have the radio position built in to them. The later cars with a steering lock mounted switch are much more reliable, if harder to access.

9 The wiper motor

The TR6 is fitted with a two-speed wiper motor, which in normal service proves to be quite reliable, although some would say its effectiveness at clearing a screen of rain is another matter. The early 6s had rocker switches as per the TR5, which operated the wipers and the screen washer. Later cars are easily identified, as the lower switch was replaced with a rotary one.

Finally, the majority of TR6s were fitted with a vertical isolator switch on the bulkhead, which is designed to cut the power in the event of a collision. By and large, they do not pose any problems but it's always worth checking it if you find you cannot start your car.

13 Trim & weather equipment

The level of trim and weather equipment fitted to TRs greatly improved during the series production run. From rather basic side screens and a separate hood on the early TRs, the models evolved into quite civilised sports cars, with wind-up windows, fitted carpets, reclining seats, and good quality Ambla upholstery. When the TR6 made its first appearance, the level of trim and weather equipment was virtually the same as the preceding TR5, with most of the trim being carried over. The most noticeable exception was the deletion of the two-piece hardtop which proved a popular option with the TR4, TR4A and TR5. This was replaced with a more angular hardtop, with fixed side and rear windows better suited to Karmann's more modern styling. More on this later.

13.1: The interior of a 1973 TR6.

Common problems

Scruffy and torn trim should be easy to spot, and the TR6 owner is fortunate in that virtually all of the trim fitted to the cars is still available. There is also a good supply of trim parts which can provide an improvement on the original offering from Triumph.

Worn out carpets are easy to replace, and even new door cards can be fitted by a DIY owner if care is taken over removing the door and window lift handles. Replacing a worn out or torn hood and tonneau cover is a more complicated affair, which *can* be done at home but is best carried out by a professional trimmer. It's important to keep the hood in good condition as any leaks will affect the interior trim. Sodden carpets and under felts can only hasten the onset of rust in the floors and sills and they will be much more expensive to replace! The Vybak plastic rear windows can become opaque, and while the large rear window can be zipped out, the two rear quarter windows are 'welded' into the hood material. There are some products available which claim to restore the clarity of Vybak windows but if they are that bad then the sensible option is to replace the hood completely.

When replacing any trim, owners have the option to upgrade their trim to whatever they fancy. Leather seats, Wilton carpets, mohair hoods, and burr walnut dashboards are all available; it just depends on your taste and the size of your wallet.

The hardtop

Depending upon the customer's preferences, the TR6 could be ordered as a fixed head coupé, a roadster, or a roadster with a hardtop. The hardtop can be unbolted and removed from the

13.4: A TR6
fitted with a
surrey top
backlight.

13.3: Storing
a hardtop
can be a
problem.

13.2: A
TR6 with
a factory-
fitted steel
hardtop.

car with relative ease, but it is advisable to have a friend with you to lift it clear of the car as, being made of steel and fitted with safety glass windows, it is quite heavy. Removal is accomplished by undoing the two bolts passing through the header rail on the windscreen, the two bolts on the inside by the B post, and the two bolts below the rear screen that secure the top to the rear deck. Refitting it is merely a reversal of the above.

There are few TR6s on the road these days that keep their hardtop on during the summer, and storage can be a problem for some owners. There are now a number of hardtop stands on the market for modern cars like the Mazda MX5 and Mercedes SLK, which may prove suitable for the TR6, so it could be worth looking into some of these if you have a storage problem. Meanwhile, some TR6 owners have resorted to fitting the

The hood and tonneau cover

The majority of TR6s sold were convertibles and came with a black Vynide hood, fitted with a zip out rear plastic window. There was also an optional full-length tonneau cover and hood cover. The hood was much more robust than those fitted on earlier models, and was quickly released from the windscreen header rail by two locking levers: a great safety improvement over the TR4A's chrome header rail locks, which could cause a nasty injury in the event of a crash. The rear quarters of the hood are held down with metal press studs on the earlier cars, but cost cutting at British Leyland saw these later replaced with black plastic studs.

The hood frame usually benefits from some lubricating oil on its many joints to aid its folding action. The TR6 also has some draught-excluding rubbers fitted to the frame. These can become loose and the rubbers do wear, so will need replacing from time

13.6: The hood on a TR6 is a snug fit.

13.5: The fibreglass hardtop is a close imitation of the factory option.

earlier two-piece type hardtop with the fixed rear screen. It is sometimes referred to as the 'surrey top,' but the 'surrey' is actually the piece of folding canvas that fits between the front and rear screens, and not the fixed backlight owners refer to. Using the fixed backlight of the TR5 does marginally improve rear vision, and it uses the same location points as the standard TR6 hardtop so is an easy conversion to do, though it's not to everyone's taste and could offend the purists who think the Karmann design is better.

As fixed surrey tops now command a very high premium, well over a £1000 for one, those who still want such a hardtop can opt for a fibreglass reproduction surrey top instead. However, when the TR6 was in series production, Karmann style fibreglass hardtops were also available on the retro-fit market (see photo 13.5).

to time. There are also Velcro strips mounted here, to which the hood can be secured. These, too, can become detached, but if everything is kept in fine fettle, the cabin of the TR6 can become a very snug place.

The hood itself benefits from regular cleaning with warm soapy water and/or vinyl cleaner. Meanwhile, the zip on the tonneau cover often gets neglected, and the press studs can become detached from the vinyl too. If the zip does break, it's worth checking out the price of a replacement zip, as it's a simple job for a trimmer, and if you can get hold of a brass one rather than a plastic one then so much the better. Failing that, Velcro could be used, but that would require another flap of material to be sewn onto the tonneau cover. Finally, it's worth noting that some tonneau covers have 'pockets' sewn in to accommodate the headrests.

Carpets

It's wise to take good care of your carpets, and regular brushing and vacuuming is all that's required on a day-to-day basis. However, if the carpets get wet then its best to remove them in order to dry them out thoroughly. As indicated above, wet and sodden carpets can introduce rust to the floor pans, so it's advisable to remove them ASAP. This is not as straightforward as it seems because removing the carpets from under the seats requires the seats and seat runners themselves to be removed first. Having said that, it's definitely worth doing, and once the seats are removed, all the other carpets become easily removable. The floor, the gearbox tunnel, and all the other carpets, are held in place by press studs and removal is easy. The carpets in the side of the footwell are held in place by screws and those along the sills are glued into position. These sill carpets should be removed with care as the carpet can tear. If this

happens, they can be fixed back into position with spray glue or similar. Leaving them in place if wet is definitely *not* a good idea! The boot also benefits from having carpet, and while the boot seal offers a good fit, leaks are not uncommon, so the same applies to the boot carpet – keep it clean and dry. Finally, if the carpets have got wet through then so, too, will the underfelts. Again, dry them well before refitting them, and if desired, some extra floor sound deadening material can be introduced at the same time.

The seats & seat belts

When new, TR6 seats were considered to be quite comfortable and were a great improvement over the earlier models. They featured a reclining mechanism operated by the chrome lever on the side and also adjustable headrests. The seats are secured by a pivot at the front, and at the rear by a spring-loaded lever which is designed to prevent the seats tipping forward during an accident. By tripping the lever, the seat can be tipped forward to access the rear shelf of the driving compartment. Another lever at the front of the underframe of the seat allows the occupant to it move backwards or forwards. Meanwhile, the headrests on TR6 can be raised into a higher position, if so desired, while some American spec cars were fitted with very high back seats that incorporated a folding headrest.

Apart from the usual tears and splits that come with use, TR6 seats last well over time. The interior foams can age harden and go to dust, and the rubber diaphragm platforms that support you can split too – if that happens you will need the services of a good trimmer.

The original pattern Ambla material is now very difficult, if not impossible, to find these days, but many owners re-trim their cars in leather, or even replace the seat completely. Mazda MX5 seats are a very popular option as they fit well and even offer built in loudspeakers! A different subframe is required if you go down this route and, of course, the tonneau cover will need work too if it is to fit over the high backs of MX5 seats.

The inertia reel seat belts fitted to the TR6 were the standard factory fitment, but some owners prefer to use a racing type harness instead, using the three seat belt anchorage points provided for each seat. The inertia reel should be checked periodically, (6000 miles or 10,000km is recommend by the factory) to see that the retardation mechanism is working

13.8: Inertia reel seat belt anchorage points.

13.9: A wooden door capping has been added to this TR6.

correctly. This can be done by driving the car to approx 15mph and then braking sharply. The seat belt should then restrain you and your passenger, but try not to throw your body forward in anticipation to activate the seat belt. The mechanism won't work like that as the harness is locked by the retardation of the car and not by body movement.

Again, being an open-topped car, the seat belts can get wet and should be allowed to dry thoroughly. If badly stained, they

13.10: The spring clips that locate this warped door casing have clearly failed.

can be cleaned with warm soapy water, but if they become frayed at all then they must be replaced.

As safety standards became more rigorous, especially so in the USA which was the TR6's main market, seat belt warning lights were fitted. These became active if an attempt was made to drive the car without the belts being used. Today, and like hazard flashers, these devices are commonplace in all cars, but back then they were something of a novelty.

Trim panels & door cards

Apart from scuffs and tears acquired over time, all of the other trim on a TR6 is easily replaced. There are two types of door cards used, the later ones being fitted to the CP series of cars, and identifiable by the recessed door closer in it. The hardboard backing of the door cards can warp over time and pull away

13.11: This is a later TR6 with a rotary wiper switch, but note the damage to the crash pad just above the speedometer.

The windscreen & wipers

TR6 windscreens were available with laminated, clear – or later on – tinted glass, and replacement screens are readily available if cracked. However, although not advertised as such, the complete windscreen assembly can also be removed from the car if so desired. It is only held in place by the three bolts on top of the dashboard, and by the two nuts underneath the dash panel. The frame is, of course, also secured with mastic to the body of the car and so removal isn't quite as easy as this suggests, but it can be done by one person with a reasonable amount of 'grunt.' Once the screen has been removed an aero screen can be fitted to deflect the bugs, but they don't really suit the modern lines of the TR6: a full-width cut down screen is a better option if you want that 'roadster' look.

Another option to consider is fitting a heated screen. I had one of the first made fitted to my own car, and in the right weather conditions, a flick of a switch produces a fully demisted screen in seconds – so much faster than waiting for some hot air to come from the engine.

The screen wipers on the TR6 are, let's face it, not really up to much. While they do offer two speeds and a screen washer mechanism, they are: a) set up for the LHD market and so don't sweep the RHD side very well; and b) not really powerful enough to clear the amount of rain the UK sees. There really isn't very much an owner can do to rectify this state of affairs, other than to keep the blades in tip top condition and make sure the springs on the wiper arms keep the blades in contact with the screen. The wiper motor on the TR6 was upgraded from that of the TR5, but it is still pretty basic and no one has yet come up with an improved system. Early TR6 wiper arms were polished metal, while later ones were satin black and the cranked arm ALWAYS goes on the right-hand side of the car looking from the driver's seat.

13.12: This wiper motor has seen better days, but at least it's easy to get at if it needs replacing.

from the door itself (see photo 13.10). Replacement is quite straightforward, but do take care when removing and refitting the inner door handles and window winders. The retaining dowel and springs can be difficult to fit. There are also two types of top rail fitting: the early type, which was carried over from the TR5 and has a finger pull moulded into it, and the later type which doesn't. If neither of these appeal, then wooden door cappings in a variety of finishes to match your dashboard are also available from various TR parts suppliers.

Other trim parts that can and do suffer are the crash pads surrounding the dashboard and the switch plinth. The H frame supporting the dash also usually shows signs of wear. Replacing the top crash pad can be relatively straightforward but it is a big time-consuming job, and with hourly garage rates being what they are, the owner of the car below could expect a very large bill to fix what is a very small but unsightly crack.

Colours

Finally, one shouldn't forget about paint and trim colours. The TR6 was often trimmed in black Ambla vinyl, but other colours of trim were available to complement the wide variety of paint colours – Tan, Red and Light Blue were popular choices. Hoods were available in black or white. As for the colour of the car itself, Triumph expanded the original range of six colours as the years progressed and tastes changed. The six original colours were Jasmine Yellow, Signal Red, Royal Blue, White, Laurel Green, and Damson, but during the TR6's production run more vibrant colours like Saffron, Emerald Green, Wedgewood Blue, Sienna Brown, Magenta, and Mallard were added.

Today, a car that's being restored can be painted and trimmed with whatever takes your fancy. The lines of the TR6 suit modern paint jobs quite well, and we are now seeing an increasing number of cars being finished in metallic colour schemes and trimmed in leather with contrasting piping. Just what Triumph would make of such things is hard to tell, but I do know that at least half a dozen TR6s were painted from new in a two-tone scheme by a well-known Triumph works dealer in Birmingham: these being Sapphire Blue and Silver, Sienna Brown and Tobacco, and Damson and Rose Pink. (It looks better than it sounds!)

13.13: One of the rare two-tone TR6s. The lighter colour was always applied above the darker one, but at least one TR6 was painted Sapphire Blue over Silver.

14 The bodyshell

The bodyshell of the TR6 was based upon that of its predecessors, the TR4 and the TR5. The very 'first' TR6 was actually fashioned by coachbuilders Karmann using a TR4 bodyshell as a pattern. They produced a very good and modern-looking facelift on what were already quite old underpinnings. It was designed to sit on a separate chassis, and unlike its counterpart, the MGB (which used monocoque construction), the TR bodyshell wasn't a stressed member, so rust or accident damage wouldn't be quite so detrimental to the car. That being said, the bodyshell does suffer from rust and in that respect the TR6 is no different from its forebears.

Common problems

Corrosion, accident damage, and poor repairs can all take their toll on a bodyshell, and signs of these can be found by looking at the panel gaps around the bonnet, boot, and the doors in particular. They should be consistent all-round with no obvious gaps; doors should open evenly and shut flush with the rest of the bodywork. The alignment of the swage line of the door with the front and rear wings is a good indicator of build and repair quality.

Bubbling paintwork is another sign that needs investigating, especially if it is along the sides of the rear deck, the lip of the boot lid, the leading edge of the rear wings and around the headlights of the front wings.

Misalignment

As the bodyshell sits on a separate chassis, all too often when a car is being restored, the body is unbolted from the chassis and lifted off, so remedial work can be carried out on the chassis. This is all well and good if the body has been supported and strengthened beforehand, but a badly rusted body will flex, and if the sills have gone there isn't much keeping the front and back halves together! For this reason, it is important to have steel braces fitted between the A and B posts. You should also leave the doors on and bolt them to the braces as well before lifting the body clear of the chassis.

Before we go on to discuss the body, there is the chassis itself to consider. Accident damage, rust, and poor repairs can seriously knock a chassis out of square. A twisted chassis

14.1: This floorpan has been removed but the A and B posts have been braced to retain strength.

only has to be out by a few degrees for the body to become complexly at odds with it, and no amount of packing will get the body to sit straight on the car afterwards. The critical areas on the chassis are around the front suspension pick-up points, the differential mountings, and the trailing arm mountings. Rust in these places can have dire consequences, with front wheels parting company from the chassis, differentials failing out, and rear trailing arms breaking away and coming adrift. None of which you want to happen when travelling at speed! Although not a cheap option, replacement chassis are available, so if your chassis is showing signs of accident damage, rust, and poor repairs then that might be a better long-term solution. And remember, early TR6s are now 50 years old – some 40 years older than the lifespan of the original design – so do think seriously about it; if in doubt, get a professional to do a drop check on the chassis to assess it for 'straightness and square.'

14.3: This box section carries the rear trailing arms.

14.2: Rust has seriously weakened this chassis.

14.4: The repaired chassis.

Bodywise, most misalignment of the panels comes about through poor sill replacement. Bearing in mind that even if genuine Stanpart panels are used, a lot of Stanpart spares were said to be seconds from the production line, and a good fit was never guaranteed. Today's reproduction panels are very good but they will still need 'fettling' in order to achieve a good fit.

The replacement of sills, floor pans, inner wings, and A and B posts is not something to be undertaken lightly, and the complete body should be assembled before final welding of the inner tub takes place. This will ensure that the outer panels will fit. Of course, if money is no object, why not opt for a new chassis and bodyshell? Although if this is the case, one should ask why you are buying the car in the first place!

14.5: Replacing the floorpan.

14.7: Running a drain pipe from the bulkhead to the wing closing panel is a good idea to prevent water ingress.

14.6: Rust here in the front wing is commonplace.

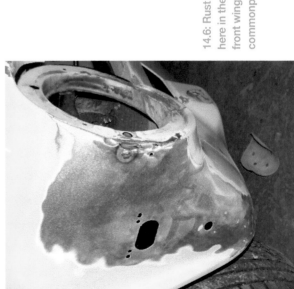

Rattles & squeaks

All TRs rattle to some extent, and my advice is to try and live with it. However, some rattles really shouldn't be there, so it's worthwhile trying to trace those and fix them. One of the worst culprits is the bonnet. Usually, it's a sign of a badly adjusted bonnet, and the rattle will manifest by the bulkhead. There are two cone-shaped rubber bonnet buffers which should fit snugly into the circular pressings in the back corners of the bonnet. These buffers are adjustable for height, so do check they are at the correct height before looking for other causes. There should also be a rubber seal at the bulkhead end of the bonnet opening, but that can be improved by fitting a larger section rubber to take up any slack. The same can apply to the boot lid too.

Doors & hinges

Doors that rattle can be down to either the window glass rattling in worn guide channels, or by badly adjusted door locks. Checks should also be made on the door and bonnet hinges. If there is too much play in them, they can produce an irritating squeak. Try oiling them first, and if that doesn't help, replacing the hinge pins should. Door hinges are adjustable on the A post when hanging doors for an initial fit, but if the door is already in place and you can lift the rear edge of the door, then the hinges ought to be replaced as the hinge pin is worn. The same test can be applied to the boot lid and its hinges.

If, when driving, you can see the gap between the door and the B pillar opening and closing, then that, too, is a sign of too much flexing of the body. First, check that all the ally body mounting washers are still in place and correctly mounted. Some movement in the bodyshell is only to be expected, but if it seems excessive, it might be advisable to check the chassis itself for corrosion.

Catches & locks

With today's cars being built by machines with millimetre precision, we have come to expect car doors to close properly and with a satisfying 'clunk' – don't expect a 50-year-old car to do the same! The door locks on the TR6 are robust and have an anti-burst feature which will prevent the door flying open in an accident. There is a certain amount of adjustment that can be made on the B post striker plate to make sure they shut properly. However, if the B post has been replaced incorrectly, then no amount of adjustment will make the door shut flush and line up with the rear wing. The external door lock has a separate barrel operated by an FS series key, which are readily available,

14.8: The emergency bonnet release cable on the right has been **wrongly fitted here. It should be on the left-hand peg.**

but modern repro barrels do not take FS keys, and in my opinion they are rather poor reproductions. Better to try and get some original barrels even if it means carrying around an extra key or two.

The same can also be said of the ignition key on the earlier TR6s, when the ignition switch was located on the dashboard plinth. Later cars were fitted with a steering column lock which can prove annoying if you have a number of keys hanging down.

The boot lock is also an FS series push lock. To open the boot, simply turn the key to unlock it and push the boot lock. Problems with the boot lock are rare.

The bonnet lock, however, is a different matter. It is cable-operated from under the dashboard, and that cable can and does break. One of the problems is that the cable run is designed for LHD cars, with the operating lever being in the wall of the LHD footwell. The cable then has to run across the whole width of the car and do a U-turn in order to operate the lever which releases the bonnet lock pin. One option is to replace the long TR6 cable with the much shorter TR4 type, which can be located on the wall of the RHD footwell.

Another option is to fit a second emergency release cable on the bonnet lock lever, and feed it down below the bulkhead where it can be accessed. A small hole may have to be drilled in the bulkhead but you can thread a cable through the Speedometer grommet.

If you are unfortunate enough to experience a bonnet release failure and do not have an emergency cable in place, then it is still possible to unlock the bonnet by drilling a small ½in diameter hole in the part of the bulkhead under the bonnet catch, and use a dowel to manually release the catch.

The lock itself is a sturdy pressed steel affair, and has a safety catch fitted to it which needs releasing when opening the bonnet. It is important to make sure the striker pin and the lock itself are properly aligned. When aligning the pin and lock, it is equally important to hold the catch in the open position, otherwise you might find yourself closing the bonnet and not being able to open it again. (I write from personal experience!)

The final lock, and one which is often overlooked, is that of the cubby box lid. It's a key-operated button affair and needs careful adjustment with its striker plate to prevent it springing open after going over every bump in the road.

14.9: A TR6 shows off its chrome.

14.10 (above) and 14.11 (left): Pitting on the TR6's chrome tail lights is commonplace. Bumpers are less prone to pitting, but they can rust.

Exterior fittings

For its age, designed when chrome ruled and cars were festooned with it like jewellery, the TR6 is remarkably restrained in this aspect; gone are the chrome beadings, side mouldings and indicator housings of the earlier TR4A and TR5. Instead, their indicators are much more discrete, and the only chrome moulding is the one on the sill. The bumpers, too, are much smoother, chunkier affairs, and they lost the overriders of the earlier cars – although later 1974 model year US spec cars did carry large black rubber overriders in order to meet US crash safety regulations. Even the grille is painted matt black, with just a single chrome bar on either side of the central TR6 badge. However, even though there is a lot less chrome, it still needs to be cared for: regular washing and the application of a proprietary chrome cleaner like Solvol Autosol will help keep the rust at bay.

Areas which do tend to get neglected are the rear tail lamp units. The lamp housing is made of Mazak and the chrome surround is susceptible to pitting, which is then very difficult, if not impossible, to remove.

Bumpers that are in too bad a condition for re-chroming can now be replaced with stainless steel ones. Door mirrors were available in two guises, either as round 'bullets' or rectangular. The rectangular door mirrors can now be sourced in black or chrome depending upon your preference. The only other bit of chrome which gets overlooked is the windscreen rubber insert. This is made of plastic, and the joint at the bottom is covered by a small chrome strip. This often gets lost and the plastic suffers from water damage. It's an easy job for any windscreen company to refit a new one for you, but downright impossible if you don't have the right tool to do it yourself!

14.12: Make a regular check under the carpets for damp and signs of rust. Note the yellow plug on the sill where rust proofer has been sprayed inside the box section.

Looking after the body

Washing accumulated road dirt off a car is easy, isn't it? You just need a bucket, lots of warm soapy water, a sponge, and a leather to dry it off afterwards – but is it really clean? Probably not.

Cleaning the underside of the car will pay greater dividends in terms of long-term ownership, and every so often it's a good idea to pressure wash the underside of the car to remove the build up of mud and debris that accumulates under the wheelarches and the front and rear wings. TR6s attract mud behind the headlamp bowls like moths to a flame, and this is a prime area for rust bubbles to start showing through. The same can be said of the rear wings.

If the car is only going to be used during the summer, it's also a good idea, at the end of the year, to remove the seats and interior carpets, and check on the condition of the floors and inner sills. This would also allow you to access the sills in order to spray some more Waxoyl inside them. And while the Waxoyl is out, why not top up the chassis members at the same time?

The real key to a rust-free car is undertaking regular maintenance and fixing any blemishes before they develop into unsightly rust scars. The moral here is if you look after your car properly then it should look after you.

There must be very few owners today who can say that their TR6 is still their everyday car. Virtually all of them have been relegated for use on 'high days and holidays.' A lot of adverts for cars proudly report that they have had 'dry summer use only,' or DSUO as is sometimes stated, but given the state of UK weather, this generally means the car has spent more time off the road than on it, which can also lead to faults and problems.

So, if your car is kept locked away in your garage waiting for the moment the sun starts to shine, here are some tips so you can be sure it will fire up for you to enjoy.

The battery

A battery that doesn't get used goes flat. Long periods of inactivity can destroy a battery if the charge in the cells falls below a certain level, so invest in a trickle charger to keep the battery topped up. The fitment of a battery isolator switch (see photo 15.1) is also a good idea because radios and clocks will still operate even if the ignition is switched off, and this switch will also prevent any short circuits.

Hydraulic fluid

Mineral-based clutch and brake fluid is hydroscopic, which means it absorbs moisture. Having water in either system is bad news, and even though the fluid should be changed at regular mileage intervals, not having the car on the road all year round means those intervals can take years to come around if you're only doing 3000 miles a year. If possible, replace the mineral

based fluid with a silicone one, but remember the two types cannot be mixed so drain the system thoroughly.

The exhaust system

A standard mild steel system will corrode from the inside even when not in use. There isn't much you can do about this apart from fitting a stainless steel system. These usually have a lifetime guarantee and if going down that route, don't forget to change the manifold as well.

15.1: A battery isolator clamp.

15.2: The date on this tyre is shown as 3308. That means it was produced in week 33 of 2008 – sometime during the week beginning 13 August, 2008.

can replenish the cooling system with distilled water, and the engine with some cheap but fresh oil. It is also a very good idea to remove the sparkplugs and squirt some engine oil into the cylinders. However, DO NOT fill them up as you risk hydraulic locking of the engine if you forget you've done so then try to start the engine. It is best to put a reminder note on the steering wheel of the car if you do. Again, with the sparkplugs removed, it is also advisable to turn the engine over BY HAND to ensure it will turn over freely. With the plugs still removed, you can then operate the starter motor in order to pump some oil around the engine.

Brakes

If you aren't going to use the car over the winter, do not apply the handbrake, as the brake linings can and will stick to the rear drums. Needless to say that if your garage is on any sort of slope, you don't want the car to roll away, so chocking the wheels will be necessary. When venturing out for the first time after a long period of inactivity, check that the brakes are actually working as the rear wheel cylinders can leak over time. If the car was put away in a wet condition, there will probably be some build up of surface rust on the inside of the brake drums and on the surface of the front discs, but this will eventually clean off under braking. Don't be surprised to hear a lot of brake squeal when this is happening.

The clutch

If the car isn't going to be used for some months, then it is highly advisable to keep the clutch pedal depressed as it's not unknown for the clutch plate to seize onto the flywheel. If that does happen, the remedy is to chock the wheels, select top gear, apply the handbrake fully, press the clutch, and operate the starter. The torque from the starter motor should be enough to free the plate, but if more than a few attempts are required and it still doesn't come free, then it might require the removal of the gearbox to free it.

The engine

If possible, do try to run the engine up to operating temperature every fortnight. If it's not possible at that regularity, once a month is an absolute minimum. If the car is going into long-term storage then it's a very good idea to drain all the oil and water from the engine – including the filter and oil cooler if one is fitted. That way any contaminates will be flushed out of the engine. You

The fuel system

Whether you have an original Lucas fuel pump or a later replacement Bosch one, it's worth energising the system once in a while to make sure it's working okay. Try not to leave too much fuel in the tank if leaving the car for long periods of time, as petrol loses its 'lights' and goes stale. I always try to add a fresh gallon or two if possible, to help with the volatility of the fuel.

Tyres

Prolonged lack of use over the winter can cause tyres to develop 'flat spots' where they come into contact with the floor of the garage. Avoid this by moving the car so that the tyres don't sit in the same position the whole time. Better still, place the car on axle stands and remove the wheels completely to stack them flat.

Also remember that tyres harden and deteriorate with age, and while a tyre might look good and have plenty of tread left, it could actually be a hazard, so do check the date stamp which is found on every tyre (see photo 15.2). There is no legal 'sell by' date, but tyre companies recommend they should be renewed every five years or so.

And finally

Before setting off on your first trip of the year do make sure that everything is working as it should be – electrics, washers, indicators, etc – and wait for the engine to get up to working oil pressure and temperature. A little patience here can save you time and money later on.

16 Competition & modification

From the very outset of the TR range of sports cars, competition was the order of the day. This was especially true of TRs in rallying in the 1950s and '60s. During the 1970s, when the TR6 was in production, the car was no longer suitable for rallying, and apart from a few diehards who raced in Modsports, it was overlooked on the race circuits too. Even so, the TR6 owner can look back and reflect upon a very good competition heritage. It is really only in more recent years that the TR6 has begun to be appreciated by the competition-minded fraternity. Meanwhile, the aftermarket sector has produced a whole host of goodies that an owner can fit to personalise their car.

When the TR6 first came out, it was in the USA that its presence on the track was really felt, and there were good reasons for this. The USA was *the* prime market for British sports cars, and the SCCA series (Sports Car Club of America) was the shop window for British Leyland and Triumph to show off its wares to an eager American public.

The TR6 was campaigned with great success by Bob Tullius, the dynamic owner and driver of Group 44 Racing. The TR6 was also the choice of Hollywood legend Paul Newman, who also raced his car with great effect.

Over in Britain, TR6s were outclassed in club racing by the likes of Lotus and TVR, so it wasn't until the advent of the various historic race series that have sprung up over the past few years that the TR6 begun to make its mark. However, the 1970s and '80s TR Register car club did a great deal to promote

6.1: A road-going TR6 built for competition.

16.2: The Group 44 TR6 as driven by Bob Tullius in SCCA racing. 40 years later it still holds a lap record at Silverstone.

competition by organising sprints and its own race championship for all types of TR, and offered classes for these six-cylinder models.

Make no mistake, though, going racing isn't cheap, and even if it's only sprints and hill climbs you decide to enter, your wallet will take a pounding. Also, it's worth noting that while your road car can be made to go faster, if you want it to be competitive then it will no longer be suitable for popping down to the shops – think carefully before you commit to preparing the car for the track!

16.3: Bob Tullius.

go faster, the first thing you should be paying attention to is your brakes. If you can brake later into a corner, then you'll be the first one out of it. After that, it's the suspension that needs looking at in order to make the car handle better. Remember, it's not top speed that counts on a race track but how you can put the power down and get through the corners.

Safety is all-important, and a proper roll cage, harness, and protective clothing are all required before starting your competition journey.

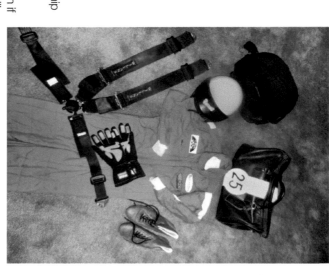

16.4: In competition, an approved harness, fireproof overalls, gloves, shoes and a helmet will help keep you safe.

Some basics

Modifying the engine is only part of the story, but it's often the one that people make the mistake of spending money on first. The simple answer is: don't. Even on a road car, if you want to ones, and while you're at it think about replacing the distributor with an electronic version. If that's all that you require from your car then so be it; if you want to turn it into more of a fire-breathing monster that can keep up with today's traffic (even a Toyota Yaris can do 100mph!), you will need to think seriously about how you are going to boost it's performance. However, before doing anything, set yourself a realistic budget and time frame to complete the work. I know of several cars that were once quite roadworthy examples, but have now been off the road for several years simply because the bar was set too high, the money ran out, and life got in the way.

Reliability

Boosting a car's performance will have an impact on its reliability. Highly tuned engines are, frankly, a pain to keep in tune, and while 200+bhp is now attainable for a TR6, ask yourself, is it worth it, and where am I going to use it? 175bhp will be just as fast on a road car and more reliable to boot.

However, fitting a more reliable modern unit like a five-speed gearbox in place of the standard overdrive one might be just the ticket. No more electrical connections to break down – which they do – and with better gear ratios, too. Purists might be offended at the loss of originality but even electric and power steering kits are now available as aftermarket parts: in themselves they might not improve mechanical reliability, but if they make the car more pleasant to drive then why not?

Servicing

The more you deviate from the original specification, the more you will pay for a service, either at your local garage or with one of the TR specialists around the country. Mechanics will have to tune and/or replace parts that are specific to your car and they

16.5: This TR6 has been tuned but is still useable on the road.

16.6: This racing TR6 has triple Weber carbs. Note the revised brake cylinders and catch tank on the bulkhead.

Think before you modify

Replacing worn out parts like shock absorbers and suspension bushes will often transform a car's handling from stodgy and lurches around corners, to a much crisper motoring experience. Similarly, if your HT leads are old and cracked, fit some new

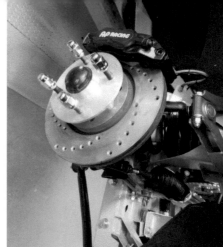

16.7: These ventilated and cross drilled discs are fitted with a four-pot brake calliper for real stopping power.

16.8: The 'Alfin' type rear brake drum shown here is actually on a TR4 but they will work equally well on a TR6.

might not be readily available, especially if they come from a competitor supplier!

Safety

Okay, so you have 200bhp under the bonnet and your car will now do 150mph. That's great, but what have you done about the brakes? Oh, you didn't have enough money left over for those Brembo brakes you had your eye on? Well, that's a shame because the next emergency stop could be into the graveyard! You cannot expect 50-year-old brakes to stop a car with 35 per cent more power. If you do upgrade the engine power, then you

16.9: This spoiler has added ducting to provide extra cooling air to the brakes.

16.11: This TR6 has been prepared for rallying. Note the navigator's foot rest and the red pull toggle to operate the fire extinguisher. The Brantz timing equipment offers accurate road and stage timing.

must improve the stopping ability. Fit larger discs and callipers first, and then look at the engine mods.

Evolutionary modifications

Not everyone wants to be on the race track, but they do want to modify their car with sensible upgrades which impart some pride of ownership in their car.

These items fall into two distinct categories; those which can improve the mechanical side of the car, and those which are purely cosmetic. On the mechanical side, this would include fitting copper and stainless steel brake pipe and hoses, pining the rear crank seal thrust washer, or fitting an oil cooler, etc. On the cosmetic side, it could be new seats and trim, a new walnut dashboard, a Mota-Lita type steering wheel, or a set of chrome wire wheels. The list is long and new products are being released all the time. The only yardstick is the size of your wallet.

In period, Triumph introduced very few modifications to the TR6. Some more obvious ones were different coloured knave

plates fitted to the wheels, Union flag stickers on the rear wings, and a chin spoiler under the front valance.

Modifying for competition

First of all, decide what level of competition you want to enter. The build spec for a sprint car will be very different for that of a race car, and even more so if you want to go rallying. The next step is to get hold of the regulations for the type of event you are interested in. These will tell you what is and isn't allowed,

16.10: This racing TR6 has a heavily modified cockpit.

16.12: High-backed rally seats with full harness and a sturdy roll cage are mandatory items in competition.

and should be read in conjunction with the RAC/MSA 'Blue Book' of motorsport regulations, and in particular Appendix K. You will also need to apply for your competition licence and join an MSA recognised club. By doing so you will be able to tap into their existing members' knowledge, thus saving you a lot of money, and they will be only too happy to welcome you into the club.

The author started his competition 'career' by sprinting his

16.13: This TR6 has been equipped with a new inlet manifold and throttle bodies for an EFI setup.

everyday TR5. As it was an everyday driver, attention was paid to make the engine produce the best of its available horsepower by carefully balancing all of the rotating parts, pistons and rods. The result was a smoothly-revving engine, which could happily exceed the original rev limit. As experience and money allowed, that was eventually replaced, with cars built with a greater emphasis on creature comfort than top speed, and later on by a purpose-built track car.

So what can be done to a TR6? The latest cars can have fully mapped injection systems, ceramic-coated exhausts, nitrided steel crankshafts, lightweight alloy hubs and radiators, dog boxes, adjustable suspension limited slip differentials, plus a host of other modifications are all available from TR specialists like

TR Enterprises, Revington TR and Racetorations, the owners of which have all competed with great success over the years in both rallying and circuit racing.

Rolling roads

Whether it'll be a race car or a fast road car, your TR6 will benefit from having a session on a rolling road. Even if you have only modified the engine with a slightly hotter cam and some gas flowing to the head and inlet/exhaust ports, a rolling road test will show you where the power is coming from and may even improve your economy. On cars fitted with much hotter cams and electronic ignition, it's false economy not to go on a rolling road, because no amount of spanner work will adjust your car as accurately as the computer can.

A rolling road measures the amount of torque being generated by the engine speed (rpm) and when divided by 5.252 it gives the amount of horsepower (bhp) at the back wheels for those revs. The difference between the two is that bhp tells you how fast you hit a tree while torque tells you how far you moved it!

16.14: A racing fuel cell has replaced the standard fuel tank on this car.

16.15: When racing, it's good to have some support with you.

16.16: Who said TRs weren't competitive?

Modifications

It is possible to modify and lighten your TR6 for competition work by fitting a fibreglass bonnet, wings and a boot lid. Couple this with a fibreglass hard top with Perspex windows and you will have saved many pounds of weight which can be used or offset elsewhere to strengthen the cars chassis and incorporate the roll cage. Needless to say, a roll cage must be secured properly, so good solid floors are vital if it is to work in an accident.

Much of what you do to your car will depend upon the regulations that are set by the organisers. In some cases, standard will mean just that, but in others, anything goes. In the UK, the TR6 was rarely seen on the race tracks. In the USA, it was a different story, with race driver Bob Tullius and the actor Paul Newman both scoring great success with their TR6 race cars.

And finally ...

The advent of classic racing has seen an increasing awareness of just how fast a TR6 can be made to go, and there are now a number of cars out there competing in a variety of events – be it hill climbing, sprinting, rallying, or racing – throughout the year. Whilst the TR6 might not be everyone's choice for a race car, especially when compared to some other classic marques, they can offer excellent value for money and that large bonnet opening makes them very easy to work on. Spares are readily available, and the vibrant club scene offers a good supporting network of enthusiasts. What's not to like?

17 Spares & tools

Probably the best spare tool that has ever been invented for the classic car owner is the mobile phone. Unless you are either very unlucky or a Luddite, no longer do you have to walk along the motorway hard shoulder to get to an emergency phone box. Help is at hand with a phone call to any of the roadside assistance companies that you might be a member of – or is it? My own experience is tempered by the fact that on the two occasions my TRs did break down neither the AA or the RAC could fix the cars. The first 'mechanic' had never even seen a carburettor before, and the other couldn't believe there wasn't a 'black box' he could plug his laptop into. Such is the world of classic car motoring in today's modern age!

Bearing in mind this sorry tale, it is therefore useful to carry a small assortment of spares and tools with you. A circular biscuit tin can fit snugly into the spare wheel and the space around it can carry all sorts of useful items. The car does come with a scissor type jack and wheel brace for changing the wheel, but that's about it. Cars that were fitted with wire wheels as standard also have a copper hammer and the large nut spanner to undo them.

What to carry with you

With just a very few exceptions, all of the nuts and bolts on a TR6 are UNF so don't bother with that nice shiny toolbox that has a wide selection of metric sockets and spanners in it. You won't need them! Toolbox essentials for me are A/F open end and ring spanners in sizes from ¼in up to 1in and the same in sockets with a ⅜in drive. Mole grips, a Stanley knife with spare

blades, a junior hacksaw, a variety of flat-blade and cross-head screwdrivers in different lengths, a hammer, some electrical wire, crimps and connectors, spare fuses, tie tags and that essential roll of duct tape. These are all sensible things to carry with you.

Spares wise, you should carry a fan belt, some jubilee clips, radiator hoses and, if possible, a water pump, as that is the most likely breakdown you can fix at the side of the road yourself without being towed to a garage. A workshop manual is very useful, and if you are going touring on the Continent, you will need a set of spare bulbs anyway.

Other electrical items worth carrying are a spare HT coil

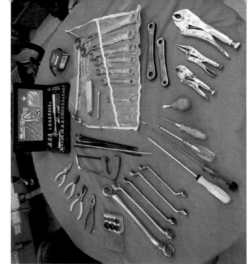

17.1: A variety of spanners, screwdrivers and pliers are all useful items, but tie wraps and duct tape are a must.

90

(you can fit it to the inner wing which keeps it handy), a set of sparkplugs, a spare distributor cap, rotor arm, points and a condenser. A thermostat and some gasket sealant would also be useful spares, but carrying things like clutch plates and brake pads is a waste of space. They should be attended to BEFORE you set out on your journey.

Some form of torch, or one of those elasticated headlamps which keep your hands free, are useful additions to any tool kit, and a spare bottle of water can help with any overheating problems. Jump leads can be useful too, but there are now compact devices on the market that can start your car and seem to have enough power to kill an elephant. If all else fails, pack a tow rope!

Back at home

Classic car owners are well known for collecting tools and spares which one day may or may not get used, but what does the average enthusiast really need in his garage?

First of all, the aforementioned workshop manual is a must. After that, a decent trolley jack and axle stands will get your car up in the air ready for you to take its wheels off so you can get at it, under and inside. Another good set of spanners, sockets and screwdrivers specifically for the garage are next – don't take the ones out of the car as you will leave them on a bench and forget to put them back in the car. Other more specialist items like torque wrenches, compression testers, air tools, and timing lights are all very well but only if you: a) know how to use them; and b) you actually do your own servicing. With air compressors being available for £100 or even less, it's a good idea to have one so you can check your tyre pressures more easily. As for other tools like arc welders and blasting cabinets, ask yourself, are they really necessary?

17.2: A copper hammer is required for fitting wire wheels and a round tin of spares fits nicely in the spare wheel.

17.3: A trolley jack, axle stands, an air compressor, and a tool cabinet are all worthwhile buys for the home garage.

Spare parts

The TR6 owner today is very well catered for, with a huge range of spare parts available from the various suppliers who specialise in the marque. Virtually everything, from a brand new chassis to a bodyshell, is now available, but while the big shiny bits are there, all too often it's that little bit of trim that's no longer supplied. This is where membership of the one of the two TR clubs comes in because, while the dealers might not have the part you are looking for, you can bet someone else does have it somewhere. The other good place to look for spares is at the various classic auto jumbles that take place up and down the country.

When replacing parts on your car, do check to see if it is the right part, and if it's a repro part make sure it is of good quality. Many repro parts are a bit dubious in this respect, rotor arms being one of the more notorious for failing. Wheel bearings, too, can be very suspect if you opt for the cheapest on the market.

Overall, it's false economy to buy really cheap parts. It's worth spending some time tracking down original old stock or even good secondhand parts rather than using the repro one.

18 The community

In 1969, the magazine *Motor Sport* published a series of letters about 'what makes a sports car.' Unsurprisingly, this generated a lot of comments from its readers, and it was generally accepted that any TR was a really good sports car, and that the TR6 would be the last of the traditional 'hairy-chested' sports cars. (The introduction of new US safety regulations were effectively

killing-off this type of open-topped car). However, one of those letters, written by one Darryl Uprichard, suggested that the early TR models were fast disappearing, and it was he who suggested a 'register' of such cars should be kept. Fast forward to January 1970, and the inaugural meeting of the TR Register took place at Hopcrofts Halt, Steeple Aston in Oxfordshire.

18.1: A gathering of TRs at Malvern Showground.

At first, the club only catered for the early side-screen cars, but long before Triumph became a footnote in history, all TRs were eligible for membership in the club.

The clubs

Today, there are a number of clubs which can offer a home for TR6 owners:

First and foremost is the **TR Register**. This should be the first port of call for any prospective or new TR owner; from here, you will be able to gain access to any one of 56 local UK groups and 23 affiliated overseas ones in Europe, South Africa, and as far away as Japan. Their office can be found at:

TR Register, 1b Hawksworth, Southmead industrial estate, Didcot, Oxon. OX11 7HR.
Tel: 01235 818866; Website: www.tr-register.co.uk;
Email: office@tr-register.co.uk

The other club which caters solely for TRs is the **TR Drivers Club**. This was founded in 1981, and was set up after a falling out between some people in the TR Register. The founders primarily hoped to cater for the later TR7 and TR8 cars but now cater for all models of TR. Chris Turner is their enthusiastic Chairman, and he is supported by a network of volunteers. The club can be contacted via info@trdrivers.com.

Catering for all sorts of Triumphs is the **Triumph Sports Six Club (TSSC)**. As its name suggests, they were formed to cater primarily for the six-cylinder Triumph models (TR6, GT6 and Vitesse) but they also take in Spitfire and Herald derivatives. They have a suite of offices in Lubenham where members can buy spares, get a coffee, and see some of the historic cars they have on display there.

Their address is:
Sunderland Court, Main Street, Lubenham, Leicestershire, LE16 9TF.
Tel: 01858 434424; Fax:01858 431936;
Email: info@tssc.org.uk

Overseas TR clubs

Standard Triumph sports cars were exported all over the world and production facilities were even set up to assemble what were known as CKD cars (Completely Knocked Down) for some models. As a result, there are strong club followings in several

18.2: Car shows like this one at the NEC are a highlight of the year for many TR clubs, allowing them to show off their members' cars.

countries around the globe, with America being home to a number of Triumph clubs.

TR6 clubs in the USA

There are a number of clubs in the USA that cater for the TR6 owner. The most noteworthy of these is the **Vintage Triumph Register** or **VTR** as it is sometimes known:

Tracing its roots back to 1973, the VTR caters for Triumph enthusiasts in the USA and Canada, and covers the diverse range of Standard Triumph cars from the prewar Standard Southern Cross, the later saloons such as the Mayflower and Standard 10, right up to the TR8. As a result, the club has over 2700 members spread all across America and in affiliated groups. Contact via their website: vintagetriumphregister.org/vtr-contact.

Buckeye Triumphs of America: Formed in 1998, this group is one of those which is affiliated with the VTR above. Contact via their website: www.buckeyetriumphs.org.

Connecticut Triumph Register: This appears to be an independent Triumph TR club, which holds a variety of meetings to the north-east of New York. Contact via email: conntriumph@gmail.com.

Detroit Triumph Sports Car Club: An off shoot of the VTR based, as its name implies, near the city of Detroit. They meet at Brass Pointe near Farmington. Contact via their website: www.detroittriumph.org.

Georgia Triumph Assn: Another VTR affiliated club based near Atlanta. Contact via their website: http://www.gatriumph.com.

Portland Triumph Owners Assn: They cover the Portland, Oregon, Washington State and Vancouver areas. Contact via their website: www.portlandtriumph.org.

Triumph Sports Car Club of San Diego: Based in sunny California, this is one of the smaller Triumph clubs in America but has an enthusiastic social following from its 120 or so members. Contact via their website: clubs.hemmings.com/sandiegotriumph.

Triumph Travelers Sports Car Club: This is another club which is affiliated with the VTR of America, and which organises events for West Coast Triumph enthusiasts. Address: Triumph Travelers Sports Car Club, Box 60314 Sunnyvale, California, CA 94088-0314; Website: www.triumphtravelers.org.

Triumph Club of Southern California: This club was originally formed in 1979, and caters for a wide variety of Triumph sports cars of all ages. Contact via website – www.sctoa.org

Australia

Triumph Car Club of the ACT (Canberra): Contact via their website: https://allancaldwell1.wixsite.com/act-triumph-car-club.

Triumph Car Club of Victoria: Contact via their website: https://www.tccv.net.

Triumph Car Club of Western Australia (Perth): Contact via their website: www.tccwa.com.

Triumph Sporting Owners Assn (Victoria): This is an offshoot of the UK TSOA, which was formed in Britain in 1953. See www.tsoavic.com.au for further details.

Manufacturers production records and archive

British Motor Industry Heritage Trust, Heritage Motor Centre, Banbury Road, Gaydon, Warwickshire. CV35 0BJ Tel: 01926 641188; Website: www.heritage-motor-centre.co.uk.

UK main spares suppliers

British Motor Heritage Ltd, Range Road, Cotswold Business Park, Witney, OX29 0YB. Tel: 01993 707200; Website: www.bmh-ltd.com.

David Manners Group, 991 Wolverhampton Road, Oldbury, West Midlands. B69 4RJ. Tel: 01215 444040; Website: www.davidmanners.co.uk; Email: enquiries@davidmanners.co.uk.

Moss-Europe, Hampton Farm Estate, Hanworth, Middlesex. TW9 6DB. Tel: 02088 672020; Website: www.moss-europe.co.uk; Email: sales@moss-europe.co.uk; Branches in London, Bradford, Bristol, Manchester, and Paris.

Rimmer Brothers, Triumph House, Sleaford Road, Bracebridge Heath, Lincoln. LN4 2NA. Tel: 01522 568000; Website: www.rimmerbros.co.uk; Email: sales@rimmerbros.co.uk.

Robsport, Unit 1-3 North End, Dunsbridge Turnpike, Shepreth, Royston. SG8 6RA. Tel: 01763 262263; Website: www.robsport. co.uk.

Revington TR, Thorngrove Barns, 10 Main Road, Middlezoy, Bridgwater. TA7 0PD. Tel: 01823 698437; Website: www.revingtontr.com; Email: info@revingtontr.com.

TR Bitz, Appleton Autodrome, Swineyard Lane, High Legh, Knutsford, Cheshire. WA16 0SD. Website: www.trbitz.com; Email: info@trbitz.com.

TR Enterprises, Dale Lane, Blidworth, Mansfield, Nottingham. NG21 0TG. Tel: 01623 793807; Website: www.trenterprises.com.

TRGB, Unit 1 Sycamore Farm Ind Est, Long Drive, Somersham, Huntingdon, Cambs. Tel: 01487 842168; Website: www.trgb.co.uk; Email: sales@trgb.co.uk.

Prestige Developments & Injection. Tel: 01978 263449; Website: www.prestigeinjection.net.

Protek Engineering, Unit 13, Bushells Business Estate, Wallingford, Oxon. Tel: 01491 832372.

USA spares supplier

The Roadster Factory, 328 Killen Road, Armagh, Pennsylvania, USA. Tel: (800) 283-3723; Website: www.the-roadster-factory.com; Email: trfmail@trfmail.com.

Forums and other useful websites

www.6-pack.org

https://www.tr-register.co.uk/forums

forum@sideways-technologies.co.uk

19 Know your TR6

Despite a decent production run lasting from 1969 to 1976, on the home market there were only ever two basic varieties of the TR6: the earlier CP series car, and the later, slightly de-tuned, CR series cars. However, within that basic outline there were a number of other small changes made during production, and of course the USA federal versions of the CC series TR6 also need to be taken into account; especially as a number of these cars are now being re-imported back into the UK and Europe.

Starting with the earlier UK home market versions, the CP series engine had the same engine as the TR5. This had a 74.7 x 95mm bore and stroke which gave it a capacity of 2498cc with a compression ratio of 9.5:1. Power was stated as being 150bhp at 5500rpm, while maximum torque was 164lb/ft at 3500rpm. When the CR series was introduced, engine power was reduced to 124bhp at 5000rpm, but as power was now being measured using the DIN system, the difference between the two power ratings is negligible on the road.

In the early 1970s, the gearbox ratios were altered slightly on 2nd, 3rd, and 4th gears to bring them in line with those used in the Stag gearbox; it was in 1973 when the A-type overdrive was replaced with a newer, lighter J-type unit. This took place from commission number CR567. About the same time, the wheels went from 5in to 5.5in rims, and an anti-roll bar was fitted to the front suspension.

Incidentally, an 'O' at the end of the commission number indicates that the car was fitted with overdrive at the factory. On cars with overdrive that don't also have the 'O,' it must have been retro-fitted.

The USA spec cars used a CC, and later on a CF, series of commission numbers. They differed quite a bit in the engine department, as they were equipped from the very beginning with Stromberg carburettors in order to pass the strict federal emissions tests. While the size of the engine remained the same as its UK counterpart, they had a lower compression ratio at 8.5:1, and could only manage 104bhp at 4500rpm. Maximum torque was even weaker with only 143lb/ft at 3000rpm.

Even tighter USA emission controls in the early 1970s saw

19.1: The engine bay of this imported LHD TR6 is now sporting a pair of SU carburettors instead of the original Stromberg units.

a further fall in compression ratios down to a lowly 7.5:1 and getting 106bhp was only possible by revving the engine to 4900rpm. Torque was also down to 133lb/ft at 3000rpm. TR6

CF1 was the first US spec car to have the new J-type overdrive fitted.

With Triumph finding it harder to meet the new federal emissions targets and safety regulations, it is surprising that the TR6 soldiered on for as long as it did. Moreover, it was still available to buy from US dealers, even when the radically different TR7 made its appearance in the USA in January 1975.

Identifying your car or a potential one

The commission plate denoting which car you have can be found on the bulkhead, and the number started with CP25001, while CR series cars started with CP1, and USA CC series cars started with CC25001, but this is only a part of the story as model years tend to complicate things.

The earliest TR6s went on sale in November 1968, and went from the aforementioned commission number CP25001. However, by using model years you get a better insight into the serial numbers used by Triumph. With grateful acknowledgement to TR historian Graham Robson, here are the relevant chassis numbers for the years the TR6 was in production:

UK and rest of the world production

1968/69	CP25001 – CP26998.
1970/71	CP5001 – CP54584
1972	CP75001 – CP77718
1973	CR1 – CR2911
1974/75	CR5001 – CR6701

19.2: The commission plate showing its CP chassis number (the last '0' shows it has overdrive), paint and trim colour numbers.

COMM.Nº CP 329700
PAINT   TRIM
GROSS LADEN WEIGHT 1380 Kg
MINIMUM KERB WEIGHT 969 Kg
MANUFACTURED BY TRIUMPH MOTORS
BRITISH LEYLAND UK LTD.
COVENTRY ENGLAND
BS.AU48 :1965 UKC 7821

19.3: This TR6 is known as 'Saffy,' and is an extremely rare and unmolested example of the marque.

USA and North America production

1969	CC25001 – CC32142
1970/71	CC50001 – CC67893
1972	CC75001 – CC85737
1973/74/75	CF1 – CF39991
1976	CF50001 – CF58328

Altogether, Triumph built 94,619 TR6s, the majority of which went to the USA, that still left some 8000+ cars here in the UK, and while there might not be that many on our roads now, the survival rate is pretty good. A decent TR6 can still be bought for reasonable money, although top condition cars are now changing hands for £30k+, while a few exceptional cars can command even higher prices.

20 Useful statistics

Period road tests are now readily available, but one question which all school-boy car enthusiasts seem to want to know the answer to is "how fast is it, Mister?" Well, the TR6 was certainly no slouch; early models could easily achieve the 120mph shown on the speedometer. Its 0 to 60mph time was also pretty good by the standards of the day, with 8.2 seconds being claimed with the use of overdrive. Fuel consumption was less of a worry in those days and 22-25mpg was also considered to be pretty good going for a car that weighed in at over a ton – 2273lb to be exact.

US spec cars were, as one might imagine, a little slower off the mark with a 10.7 second dash to 60mph.

Engine

Six cylinders:	74.7mm bore x 95mm stroke (2.9in x 3.74in)
Cubic capacity:	2498cc (152in³)
Compression ratios:	UK 9.5:1
	USA 7.75:1 or 7.5:1 (Varies with model year)
Valve clearances:	0.25mm (0.010in) (when set cold)
Valve timing:	Inlet and exhaust open equally at Top Dead Centre (TDC)
Fuel system:	Lucas Mk 2 high pressure mechanical fuel-injection fed by Lucas electric pump

Note: US spec cars use an AC mechanical fuel pump to feed twin side draught Stromberg 175CDSE carburettors. These were later changed to 175CDSE2 in 1971/72, and afterwards to 175CDSEV for the last four years of TR6 production.

Dimensions

Overall Length:	12ft 11in (3937mm)
Width:	4ft 10in (1470mm)
Height:	with hood up: 4ft 2in (1270mm)
	with hood down: 3ft 10in (1170mm)
Wheelbase:	7ft 4in (2240mm)
Track:	front: 4ft 2¼in (1276mm)
	rear: 4ft 1¾in (1264mm)
Ground clearance:	6in (152mm)
Turning circle:	34ft (10.4m)

Weights

Dry:	2280lb (1034kg)
Wet:	2390lb (1084kg)
Max gross weight:	2960lb (1342kg)
Vehicle capacity weight:	412lb (187kg)

Capacities

	Imperial	Metric	USA
Fuel tank:	11.25 gallons	51 litres	13.5 gallons
Engine sump:	9 pints	5.11 litres	10.8 pints
Gearbox:	2 pints	1.13 litres	2.4 pints
O/D gearbox:	2.66 pints	1.5 litres	3.2 pints
Rear axle:	2.25 pints	1.42 litres	2.7 pints
Cooling system (including heater):	11 pints	6.2 litres	13.2 pints

Tyres & pressures

185SRx15

Front: 20lb/in²	Rear: 24lb/in²
Front: 1.41kg/cm²	Rear: 1.69kg/cm²

Ignition system

Coil:	Lucas HA12
Distributor:	Lucas 22D with centrifugal advance & vacuum retard
Contact gap:	0.015in (0.4mm)
Firing order:	1 – 5 – 3 – 6 – 2 – 4
Sparkplugs:	Champion UN-12Y with 0.025in (0.63mm) gap
Ignition timing:	Static: 12 degrees BTDC
	Idle: 4 degrees ATDC

Electrical system

Voltage:	12v Negative Earth. 35 amp fuse box
Alternator:	Lucas 17 ACR with integral control unit and 36 amps nominal output
Battery:	Lucas 57 amp hour with 5 amp charging rate
Starter motor:	Lucas M100 pre-engaged type
Flasher unit:	Lucas 8FL 3.6 amp
Hazard unit:	Lucas 9 FL 10A max
Fuel and temp gauges:	Smiths bi metal resistance 10 volts system.

Braking system

Girling tandem hydraulic system with direct-acting servo.

21 Troubleshooting

Below are some typical symptoms you may encounter, with their probable cause and the remedies you should investigate:

Symptom	Possible cause	Potential remedy
Engine		
Engine will not crank	There is a fault in the starting system	Refer to section on electrics
Engine cranks slowly	Engine oil too thick; stiff engine after rebuild; engine seized	Drain and replace oil; strip engine and replace parts as required
Engine cranks but does not start	Fault in ignition system; fault in fuel system; incorrect valve timing; compression leak	Re-time the engine; check head gasket
Engine starts but only runs for short periods	Air leak in manifold; blockage in exhaust	Trace and seal leak; remove blockage
Engine misfires at low speed	Fault in ignition or fuel systems; air leak in manifold; poor valve seating	Trace and seal leak; regrind valves
Engine misfires at high speed	As above but valves may be sticking	Free valve and trace cause
Engine misfires on acceleration	As above but investigate for a broken valve spring	Trace and replace springs
Rough idle	Leaking head gasket; incorrect tappet clearances; worn cylinder bores	Replace gasket; adjust tappets; replace pistons and rings
Excessive oil consumption	Leaking oil seal; worn valve guides or piston rings	Replace seal or guides; fit new piston rings
Excessive fuel consumption	Fault in fuel system	Refer to fuel page
Pinking	Fault in fuel or ignition systems	Refer to those pages

Symptom	Possible cause	Potential remedy
Ignition system		
Engine cranks but does not start	Battery discharged or defective; contact breaker points failure; sparkplugs defective	Recharge or replace battery; clean or replace points and/or sparkplugs
Engine starts but only runs for short periods	Possible short to earth or loose connection	Check plug leads and all connections
Engine misfires at low speed	Wrong type of sparkplug fitted	Clean, re-gap or replace sparkplugs
Engine misfires at high speed	Open circuit or loose connection in LT circuit	Trace and rectify
Engine misfires on acceleration	Plug leads connected wrong	Check firing order
Rough idle	Static timing incorrect	Re-time ignition
Engine runs rough at high speed	Contact breaker points failure	Replace points
Lack of power	Coil or capacitor breaking down	Replace
Poor acceleration	Open circuit or loose connection in LT circuit	Trace and rectify
Lack of top speed	HT circuit broken in distributor due to damp	Clean and dry distributor cap
Excessive fuel consumption	Vacuum advance not working or worn distributor	Rectify or replace
Pinking	Using wrong grade of fuel	Boost the octane rating to 98–100
Lubrication & cooling system		
Excessive oil consumption	Worn pistons and rings; worn valve guides; leaking crank oil seal or oil filter and cooler	Rebore, hone and fit new oversize pistons and rings; replace valve guides and/or seals
Low oil pressure	Faulty gauge pressure switch or relief valve; worn oil pump or oil pick up blocked; damaged main or big end bearings; crank oil seal defective	Test and replace as required; replace oil pump; check crank and renew main bearings as required; replace oil seal

Symptom	Possible cause	Potential remedy
Overheating	Lack of coolant, thermostat jammed; fan belt slipping; radiator core clogged with debris; water pump failure	Check coolant level; replace thermostat; check fan belt tension; clean and flush radiator core; replace water pump
Engine fails to get to temperature	Thermostat jammed open	Replace thermostat
PI fuel system		
Engine cranks but does not start	Empty fuel tank; blockage in fuel line; fuel pump not working	Fill tank! Blow fuel lines through; check electrical fuse on pump
Engine starts but only runs for short periods	Fuel and/or air filter blocked	Replace filters as necessary
Fuel pump making excessive noise	Cavitation in pump	Replace pump or fit a cooling coil
Fuel pump running hot	Overheating bearing	Replace pump or fit a cooling coil
Engine 'hunts' at low speed	Excessive use of choke	Close choke
Engine misfires at high speed	Air leak on manifold	Trace and seal leak
Engine misfires on acceleration	Throttle linkage badly adjusted	Adjust linkage and air bleed valve
Rough idle	Idling speed too low; pressure relief valve sticking	Increase throttle speed air flow mixture; check PRV
Excessive fuel consumption	Choke left open; metering unit malfunction	Close choke; check metering unit
Backfiring	Blockage in fuel line; air leak at inlet manifold	Clear blockage with airline; trace and seal leak
Clutch & gearbox		
Clutch slipping	Clutch plate face worn; broken pressure plate	Replace clutch plate; replace clutch cover
Clutch will not disengage	Low clutch fluid or air in the system; slave linkage bent or faulty	Top up clutch fluid and bleed system; straighten or renew linkage
Clutch judder	Clutch plate warped	Replace clutch plate

Symptom	Possible cause	Potential remedy
Clutch noise, squeal	Release bearing breaking up	Replace bearing
Clutch noise, rattles or chatters when idling or engaging	Loose clutch or drive plate	Replace clutch
Car jumps out of gear when accelerating	Worn layshaft	Rebuild gearbox
Gearbox makes rattling noise	Synchro cones worn	Rebuild gearbox
Overdrive won't engage	Break in electrical circuit; failure of o/d oil pump	Check all wiring; check the detent switches on the top cover are adjusted properly; check oil level in gearbox and repair pump if required
Overdrive solenoid works but overdrive doesn't	Solenoid not actuating the lever correctly	Check adjustment on solenoid lever

Steering

Symptom	Possible cause	Potential remedy
Steering is stiff	Lack of lubricant in steering gear; incorrect steering geometry; uneven tyre pressures; wheels out of alignment	Grease steering; check geometry; check tyre pressures; adjust toe in and camber angles
Steering feels loose	Worn steering joints	Check all ball joints and steering couplings
Wheel shimmy	Slack wheel bearings; loose wheel nuts; steering rack loose	Check all wheel bearings; tighten steering rack mountings if loose; check all road wheel nuts and wire wheel splines are torqued up correctly
Car pulls to one side	Brakes pulling to one side; shock absorbers defective; broken spring; chassis frame twisted	Check brakes, springs and shock absorbers mountings; carry out drop check on chassis
Excessive tyre wear	Wrong tyre pressures; wheels out of balance or alignment; worn steering joints	Check pressures; replace tyres and get wheels balanced; check steering joints

Symptom	Possible cause	Potential remedy
Brakes		
Brake failure	Fluid leak; seized brake pistons; air in the system; defect in master cylinder	Check for leaks at all unions; free and clean pistons; bleed brakes; replace master cylinder
Brakes ineffective	Worn brake pads and linings; worn or scored discs and drums	Replace all as required
Brakes grab to one side	Loose calliper or back plate	Check and tighten bolts accordingly
Rear brakes binding on	Broken spring on drums	Check and replace
Spongy brake pedal	Air in the system; low brake fluid; calliper, master or wheel cylinders defective	Bleed system; top up fluid; replace parts as required
Excessive pedal travel	Brake servo failure; wear in linkage; callipers or wheel cylinder defective	Replace defective parts
Hard to press pedal	Brake servo failure; wear in pedal linkage; blockage in pipework	Check servo vacuum hose for leaks; replace servo; check pedal mechanism; clear blockage
Brake squeal	Pistons in callipers or cylinder seized; brake pads not returning	Free up pads/linings and clean; grease shim plates with copperease
Shuddering under braking	Callipers or back plates loose; disc rotor scored or warped	Check fixing bolts and tighten; replace discs if needs be.
Handbrake ineffective	Brake shoes worn or badly adjusted; brake drums worn; cables worn	Check and either adjust or replace parts
Electrical equipment		
Starter fails to crank engine	Battery discharged; starter motor solenoid defective; starter pinion jammed in ring gear	Charge or replace battery; replace starter motor; remove starter motor and check operation and condition of ring gear
Starter only cranks engine slowly	Battery discharged; bad earth; pre-engaged starter unit failing	Charge or replace battery; check earthing; replace starter motor

Symptom	Possible cause	Potential remedy
Ignition warning light remains on above idle speed	Loose connection; fan belt slack; alternator defective	Check wiring; tighten fan belt; replace alternator
Ignition warning light doesn't come on	Battery discharged; bad earth; broken or loose connection; bulb burned out	Recharge or replace battery; trace bad connection; replace bulb
Ignition warning light stays on even when engine is turned off	Ignition switch defective; alternator defective	Replace switch; check alternator wiring
Headlights dim	Alternator defective; light switch defective	Replace diode pack or complete alternator; replace light switch
Headlights fixed on dip or main beam	Dip switch broken	Check for loose connection otherwise replace
Indicators malfunction	Relay malfunction	Check earth connection or replace relay

Also from Veloce –

ENTHUSIAST'S RESTORATION MANUAL™

How to restore

Triumph TR5/250 & TR6

YOUR step-by-step colour illustrated guide to body, trim & mechanical restoration

Roger Williams
Foreword by Bill Piggott

REVISED & UPDATED EDITION

This step-by-step guide to planning and restoring your car in the most cost-effective way. Includes body, trim and mechanical restoration, left- to right-hand drive conversion, clubs, specialists and suppliers, welding and restoration techniques, and advice on what work to sub-contract.

ISBN: 978-1-787113-43-5
Paperback • 27x20.7cm • 192 pages • 450 colour pictures

The Essential Buyer's Guide

200,000 COPIES SOLD THIS SERIES

TRIUMPH
TR6
1967 to 1976

TRIUMPH

Your marque expert: Roger Williams

Don't buy a car without this unique illustrated guide! Expert advice will help you to find the best car for your money.

ISBN: 978-1-787116-58-0
Paperback • 19.5x13.9cm • 64 pages • 101 colour pictures

For more information and price details, visit our website at www.veloce.co.uk
email: info@veloce.co.uk • Tel: +44(0)1305 260068

Also from Veloce –

ISBN: 978-1-787112-89-6

ISBN: 978-1-787110-77-9

ISBN: 978-1-845848-54-5

For more information and price details, visit our website at www.veloce.co.uk
email: info@veloce.co.uk • Tel: +44(0)1305 260068

Index